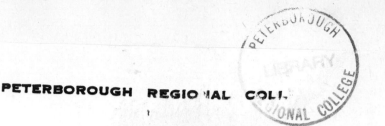

Atlas of World Affairs

The economic, social and environmental systems of the world are in turmoil. The last few years have seen possibly irrevocable change in the politics of Europe and Asia, the environment of Africa and Latin America, the economies of the Pacific Rim and the position of America as power broker to the continents. Entirely revised and updated, this atlas describes the people, factions and events that have shaped the modern world from the Second World War up to and including 1990.

International issues and conflicts are placed in their geographical context through the integration of a hundred maps. The political context provided for current events will be invaluable to all those uncertain about the development of the Khmer Rouge, what Zaire used to be called, where the 'four little dragons' are or even about the currency of Ecuador. Material on new issues includes environmental concerns, the Iran–Iraq war, the invasion of Kuwait, the Soviet withdrawal from Afghanistan, events in Panama and Columbia and the changing map of Europe and the USSR.

Revised and in print since 1957, *An Atlas of World Affairs* has proved a valued guide for the student, teacher, journalist and for all those interested in post-war political history and current affairs.

Andrew Boyd began his acquaintance with international affairs in 1946, when as a British liaison officer he attended the very first sessions of the United Nations (his other books include three about the UN). He has travelled widely and reported on international affairs while writing on world affairs for *The Economist* for 37 years.

ANDREW BOYD

An Atlas of World Affairs

NINTH EDITION

LONDON AND NEW YORK

First published 1957 by Methuen & Co. Ltd
Second edition 1959
Third edition 1960
Fourth edition 1962
First published by Methuen as a University Paperback (fifth edition) 1964
Sixth edition 1970
Seventh edition 1983
Reprinted 1985

First published by Routledge (eighth edition) 1987
Reprinted 1989, 1990

Ninth edition published 1991
by Routledge
11 New Fetter Lane, London EC4P 4EE

Simultaneously published in the USA and Canada
by Routledge
a division of Routledge, Chapman and Hall, Inc.
29 West 35th Street, New York, NY 10001

Typeset in 10/12pt Ehrhardt by Leaper & Gard Ltd, Bristol
Printed and bound in Great Britain by
Biddles Ltd, Guildford and King's Lynn

British Library Cataloguing in Publication Data

Boyd, Andrew, 1920–
   An Atlas of World Affairs/Andrew Boyd–9th edition
   Includes index
   ISBN 0-415-06624-7   ISBN 0-415-06625-5
   1 World politics–1945–Maps 2 Historical geography–Maps
   I. Title
   G1035.B6   1992   (G&M)
   911–dc20

Library of Congress Cataloging in Publication Data
has been applied for

Contents

Notes

An italic number in brackets – e.g. *(44)* – is a cross-reference. The number refers to a map and its accompanying note, not to a page. So do the entries in the index.

Distances are expressed in miles. One mile is roughly 1·61 km. One nautical mile is roughly 1·85 km. To convert square miles into square km, multiply by 2·59. The tonne and the ton are roughly equivalent.

For the sake of brevity, the United Kingdom of Great Britain and Northern Ireland is usually called Britain; the Union of Soviet Socialist Republics may be the USSR or the Soviet Union; the United States of America is often the USA or the US, the United Nations the UN; the Netherlands is usually named as Holland, and so on. Many acronyms and other abbreviations are used. Most of them are explained where they occur; others are listed here (translated into English where required).

FNLA	Angola National Liberation Front
Frelimo	Mozambique Liberation Front
Fretilin	Timor National Liberation Front
GUNT	Transitional Government of National Unity (in Chad)
KGB	State Security Committee (political police in USSR)
MPLA	People's Movement for the Liberation of Angola
Polisario	People's Liberation Front of Sakia el Hamra and Rio de Oro (in Western Sahara)
Renamo	Mozambique National Resistance
SWAPO	South West Africa People's Organization (in Namibia)
UNITA	National Union for the Total Independence of Angola

1 People and pressure

The human race has more than doubled its numbers in the past half-century. In 1940 there were about 2,250 million people. Now there are about 5,400 million. The number being added each year is reckoned at about 90 million. So the 6,000 million mark will be passed during the 1990s.

The two biggest masses of people – in China, and in the group made of India, Pakistan and Bangladesh – are both in Asia. Asia has probably always contained more than half the human race. Asia and Africa together contain more than two-thirds of it. Adding Latin America to them and subtracting Japan, the 'third-world' countries (7) contain about three-quarters. And this proportion is rising, because third-world rates of population

growth are relatively high – in spite of the effects in some areas of tropical diseases, recurrent food shortages and even famines. By contrast, in some European countries natural growth has ceased (although immigration has kept population figures rising).

Growing at 2% a year, a population doubles in 35 years; at 3.5%, it doubles in 20 years. Many third-world countries' populations were growing at annual rates between 2% and 3.5% in the 1980s. More than half of the world's countries have adopted policies aimed at limiting population growth, but the results have varied widely. Some governments, and some religions, have discouraged the limiting of family sizes. Some countries' rulers have encouraged the raising of large families in order to increase military manpower.

More people means more pressure on natural resources: deforestation, soil erosion, overgrazing, the enlargement of deserts; at sea, overfishing; in fast-growing cities, the multiplication of crowded slums.

The growth of giant cities is a feature of our time. In 1950 there were only six cities or conurbations that had as many as 5 million inhabitants

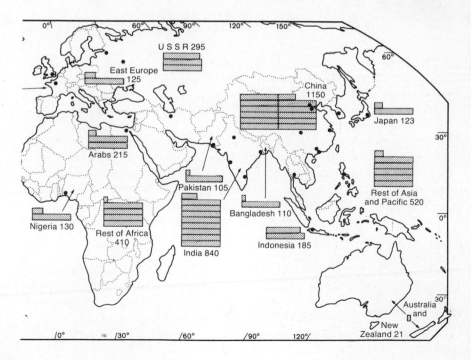

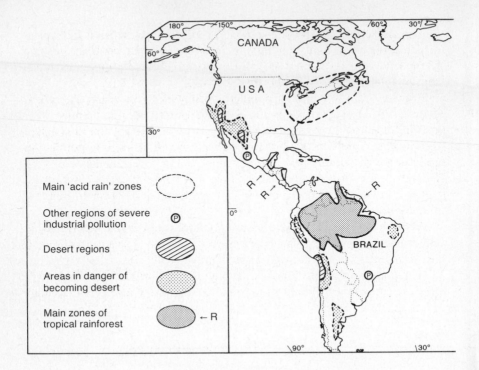

Main 'acid rain' zones

Other regions of severe industrial pollution

Desert regions

Areas in danger of becoming desert

Main zones of tropical rainforest ← R

each. Now there are more than 30, and most are in third-world countries; taking a few examples, Mexico City has 20 million inhabitants, Calcutta 12 million, Teheran 10 million. There are about 200 cities with a population of more than one million.

Over population is not the only cause of the loss of forests and growth of deserts. Ill-chosen government policies often play a part. Misdirected subsidies have encouraged deforestation in Brazil and other countries. In the 1950s China's Maoist rulers enforced a 'great leap forward' which, as well as causing millions of deaths, deforested and desertified huge tracts of central Asia. In the late 1980s Soviet planners' disastrous errors were still enlarging the desert region around the Aral Sea (and drying up that sea itself).

Forests have also been destroyed by the form of industrial pollution called 'acid rain'. Mainly caused by the burning of coal and oil, industrial pollution can not only create local health hazards; it can also, in the form of 'greenhouse gases', affect the whole world climate, producing a global warming – with a rising sea level among the side effects. (The greenhouse

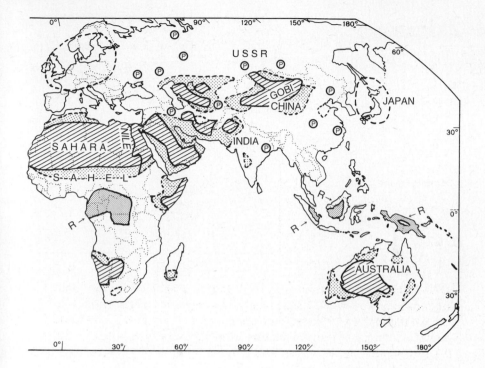

gases include the man-made chlorofluorocarbons, which, additionally, are damaging the layer of ozone in the stratosphere that protects the Earth from harmful ultra-violet rays. There is already a hole in the ozone layer above the Antarctic, *12.*)

Forests, left intact, absorb carbon dioxide; burning them produces it; thus deforestation can intensify the 'greenhouse effect' twice over. While most experts now agree in predicting a global warming, forecasts of its pace, scale and effects vary; but, according to widely accepted calculations, it is already too late to avert it completely. However, attempts to limit the damage to the ozone layer have begun, and there is now international concern about the need to preserve what remains of the big tropical rain forests. One new approach is a series of offers to relieve third-world countries of part of their foreign debt if they will adopt specific measures to protect the environment.

2 Power

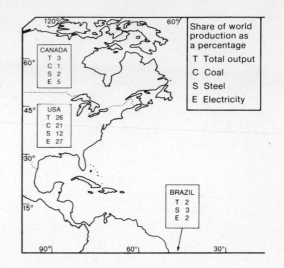

Share of world production as a percentage

T Total output
C Coal
S Steel
E Electricity

About three-quarters of the world's output is produced by the United States, Japan, the USSR, Canada and the 12 member states of the European Community (*19*). These countries contain only a fifth of the world's population. Together with China, they form a group which, with two-fifths of world population, produces about three-quarters of world output of coal, steel and electricity.

Although oil and nuclear energy (*3, 4*) may make more headlines, steel, coal and electricity are also pointers to the distribution of economic power. Recent years have seen steel output falling in the USA and Europe – partly because of more output in third-world countries (*5, 7*), partly because of recession linked with oil price rises (*3*). But those same price rises spurred on increases in coal production in many places.

The governments that take part in the annual 'economic summit' meetings held since 1975 by the major non-communist industrialized states are those of Britain, Canada, France, Germany, Italy, Japan and the United States. The major west European countries cannot, as separate states, come anywhere nearer matching American economic power; but their combination in the 12-member European Community makes up an entity more comparable with the USA. Within their group, German economic power has become prominent, and in 1990, after the uniting of West and East Germany, it was generally assumed that this prominence would increase – although, at first, the task of getting the East German economy on to its feet after 45 crippling years of communist control would impose a heavy burden on the Germans (*18*).

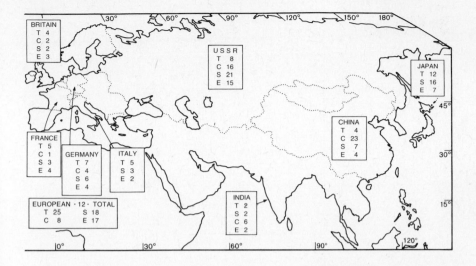

The most striking recent advance has been made by Japan. It has to import nearly all its oil, coal and iron ore, and its population is only half that of the USA or the USSR, but it has achieved the world's second biggest national output, has raised its standard of living to a 'western' level and has competed so successfully in export markets that it has built up huge trade surpluses (*57*). In terms of shares of world output, Japan's rise has been roughly equal in scale to the USSR's fall. During the 1980s the inefficiency of the Soviet economic system became so painfully clear that Soviet foreign policy was strongly influenced; the USSR found that it needed western co-operation and that it could no longer subsidize such third-world states as Cuba, Angola and Vietnam (*34, 60, 69*).

A list of all the countries whose economic power gives them international influence would include some major oil exporters. The influence of some Arab states, in particular, has been increased by their oil output (*3, 40*); and 65% of the world's known reserves of oil are in the Middle East and North Africa. However, about 80% of its reserves of coal are in North America, Europe, the USSR and China.

3 Oil

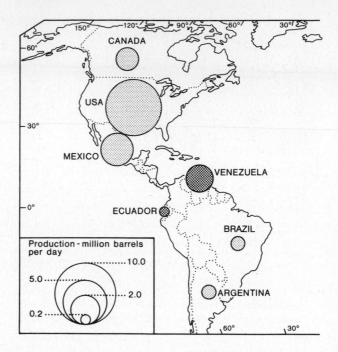

In the 1960s coal was succeeded as the world's biggest source of industrial energy by oil (petroleum) and the natural gas that is often found with it. World production of crude oil, which had been 275 million tons in 1938, rose to 1,050 million tons in 1960, to 2,275 million in 1970 and to 3,100 million in 1979.

The upsurge was then checked. Oil output fell by 10% between 1979 and 1981. This was a reaction to the startling increases in oil prices during the 1970s. Prices roughly tripled in 1973–4, and tripled again in 1978–80. In both cases the rises were linked to turbulence in the Middle East. The effects were most acutely painful for those third-world (7) countries that produced no oil, but inflation and recession hit even the richest industrial states. Total demand for energy stopped growing in many places and even fell in some. Where they could, consumers switched from oil to other sources of energy.

Before the 'oil shock' years the pattern had been changing rapidly. In 1960 a third of all oil output was in the USA, 14% each in the USSR and Venezuela, and only a quarter in the Middle East and North Africa. But Middle East oil was easy to extract and thus cheap. By 1970 the output

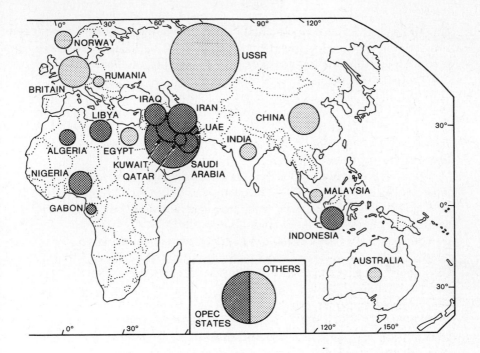

figures were already: Middle East and North Africa 40%, USA 21%, USSR 16%, elsewhere 23%. Europeans, and to some extent Americans, had become worryingly dependent on oil from Arab states and Iran.

During the 1960s the Organization of Petroleum Exporting Countries (OPEC) was formed (members, in 1990: Algeria, Ecuador, Gabon, Indonesia, Iran, Iraq, Kuwait, Libya, Nigeria, Qatar, Saudi Arabia, United Arab Emirates, Venezuela) and the members of this 'cartel' began to try to raise prices by joint pressure. Their strength was suddenly increased by the 1973 Arab–Israeli war (*43*), when Arab states cut oil sales to some western countries for a time. Prices soared, and national economies sagged – except in the oil-exporting states. The second big wave of price rises began in 1978, when Iran's exports were sharply reduced during the turbulent last months of the Shah's rule (*47*). But by 1981 the market was shrinking, and prices, as well as sales, began to fall.

The 1980–8 war between Iraq and Iran had remarkably little effect on world oil output or prices. The steep fall in prices in 1986 was caused by Saudi Arabia's decision to step up output, after keeping it for several years at a level far below the huge Saudi capacity. In 1990 Iraq's invasion of

15

Kuwait, and the angry international reactions, brought a quick price increase; but within a few months prices had fallen back again, and other producers had filled the gap created by Iraq's inability to sell oil in the face of a United Nations embargo (*45*).

World oil consumption in 1990 was little more than in 1979, at the end of the great upsurge. The OPEC cartel's share of world output had fallen from 48% to 36%. OPEC's price rises had spurred on exploration and production in many other countries, including Britain, whose North Sea fields had made it a net exporter.

There had been predictions that OPEC's strength would revive in the 1990s, thanks to the large Middle Eastern share of known oil reserves (25% in Saudi Arabia, 10% each in Iran, Iraq and Kuwait). But Iraq's 1990 aggression split the Arabs and, consequently, OPEC.

The map shows only a limited number of oil-producing countries. Lesser producers include Angola, Bahrain, Bolivia, Brunei, Burma, Cameroon, Chile, Colombia, Congo, Ivory Coast, Oman, Peru, Syria, Trinidad, Tunisia, Turkey and Yemen (*7*). Some large-scale producers are, nevertheless, net importers, e.g. Brazil, India and, most conspicuously, the United States. South Africa has undertaken production of oil from coal. Brazil, since the 1970s, has got one-third of its 12 million motor cars running on alcohol (ethanol, made from the sugar-cane crop).

Natural gas has, in recent years, provided the world with an amount of energy roughly equal to half that of all the oil produced. Holland, Italy, New Zealand and Pakistan are among the countries whose gasfields are of special importance to them because they have little or no oil. Until the 1960s nearly all the gas used was moved through pipelines and, apart from deliveries from Canada to the USA, it was distributed mainly within the countries where it was found. Today special tankers carry liquefied natural gas (LNG) across the sea (the biggest traffic being to Japan from Australia, Indonesia and Malaysia), and pipelines from the USSR take gas to countries in both eastern and western Europe.

4 Nuclear geography

Since 1956, when the world's first commercial-scale nuclear reactor began to contribute to Britain's electricity supplies, nuclear power plants have been built in most of the industrialized countries and in several third-world ones (7). So far, they are producing about 15% of the world's electricity, but the proportion is much higher in some countries, e.g. France, Sweden and Switzerland.

Proposals to use more nuclear energy have aroused sharp controversy in some western countries. Decisions to use it have been encouraged by fears about eventual exhaustion of the world's oil and coal, about the pollution caused by burning those 'fossil fuels' and, more recently, about a 'greenhouse effect' leading to a global warming (1); alarm about the risks involved has worked the other way. Much depends on solving the problem of disposing of dangerous reactor waste. The 1986 disaster at the USSR's Chernobyl plant, 70 miles north of Kiev (14), which spread radioactivity across Europe, led to increased anxiety.

All the nuclear power hitherto produced has come from uranium. (To use lighter elements would require the harnessing of controlled processes of nuclear fusion, not fission.) Uranium has been found in many places but is often thinly dispersed and costly to extract. Sweden, with huge reserves, has found it cheaper to import fuel for its reactors; and much of South Africa's uranium has been extractable at a competitive price only as a by-product of gold mining. The biggest known reserves of richer uranium ores are in Australia, Canada, Niger and the USA. During the 1980s the biggest recorded production was in the USA, Canada, South Africa, Australia, Namibia, France and Niger. (China and the USSR keep their figures for uranium output and reserves secret.)

Fear that wider use of nuclear energy might bring wider access to nuclear weapons helped to produce the 1968 Nuclear Non-proliferation Treaty (NPT), aimed at limiting that access to the five countries which already had such weapons. Three of the five (Britain, USA, USSR) undertook not to help other states to acquire nuclear arms; the other NPT states (138 by 1990) agreed that the International Atomic Energy Agency (IAEA) should inspect their nuclear installations and see that no material was diverted into making weapons. But nuclear-armed China and France

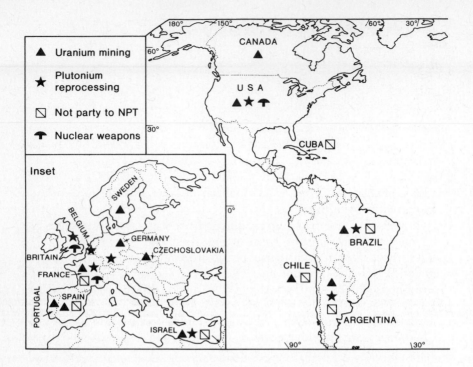

refused to sign the treaty, and the other non-signatories include several states that are regarded as 'near-nuclear'. Argentina, Brazil and South Africa have worked secretly towards developing nuclear weapons. India, which set off a test explosion in 1974, was believed to have constructed several nuclear weapons by the end of the 1980s. In 1990 the Americans suspended their aid to Pakistan because they could not be sure the country had not acquired nuclear arms. Pakistan had repeatedly been detected trying to import relevant kinds of equipment. So had Iraq (although it was an NPT signatory). A reactor near Baghdad, which France was supplying with highly enriched uranium, was attacked in 1981 by aircraft from Israel, which accused Iraq of trying to acquire bomb material. Israel itself was widely believed to have produced material for nuclear weapons.

An atomic bomb may be made either with highly enriched uranium or with plutonium. All reactors produce plutonium; but, before a weapon can be made from it, it has to be separated out from the used reactor fuel by reprocessing. Few countries have the necessary reprocessing plants as yet – but those few include several 'near-nuclear' states.

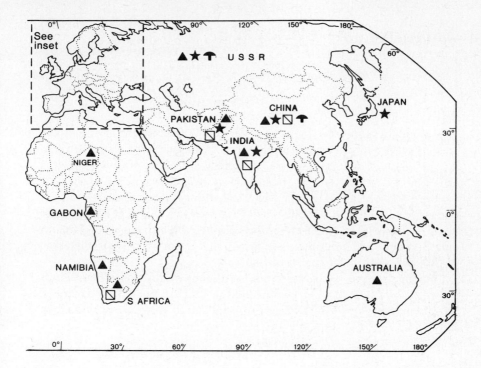

5 Some key minerals

Coal, oil and uranium (2–4) are not the only mineral resources that can give a country special significance. There are a number of minerals which are not sources of energy but are concentrated in a few areas to a degree that can have important consequences, both economic and political.

For example, Brazil, Bolivia, Malaysia, Indonesia and Thailand have in recent years produced more than half of the world's output of tin – a metal used for many other purposes besides canning. Australia, Guinea, Jamaica and Surinam have produced more than half the world's output of bauxite, the ore from which aluminium is made.

Among the ferro-alloys, which are used in the production of many kinds of steel, two-thirds of all nickel is mined in Canada, the USSR, Australia, Indonesia and New Caledonia; nearly half of all tungsten (wolfram), in

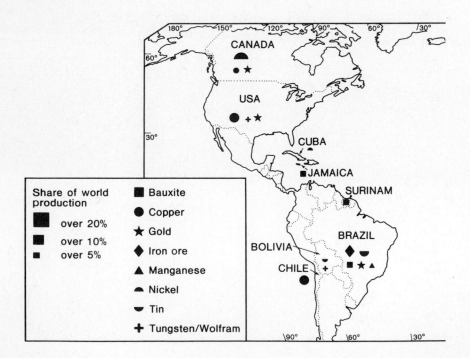

China and the USSR; two-thirds of all manganese, in the USSR, South Africa and Gabon. Not marked on the map are chrome (major producers: USSR, South Africa, Albania, India, Finland, Zimbabwe) and cobalt (Zaire, USA, Zambia, Canada, Morocco, Finland).

South Africa and the USSR are the biggest sources of platinum and gold, and, together with Australia, Botswana and Zaire, of diamonds. Both gold and diamonds have industrial uses, but gold's main role in the world economy is still that of serving as a form of monetary reserve – so, when international tension rises and confidence in national currencies is weakened, the price of gold is likely to rise, to the benefit of the exporting countries.

New developments can change a map such as this one quickly and dramatically. Australia's appearance among the foremost mining states, for example, is a quite recent development (although the country has shared California's fame during the mid-nineteenth-century 'gold rushes'). If this map had been produced in the 1960s it would have shown no markings on that country.

Western Europe and Japan are not well endowed with the minerals

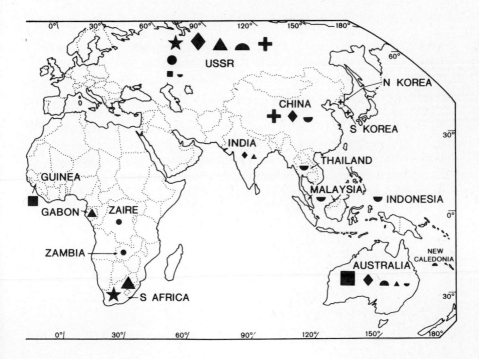

marked on the map – although, in recent years, small percentages of the world's bauxite have come from France and Greece; of its copper, from Japan, the Scandinavian states and Spain; of its iron ore, from Britain, France, Norway, Spain and Sweden. (Sweden used to be a much more prominent source of iron ore than it is now.) In general, European and Japanese industries depend heavily on imported materials. And, while much processing of those materials has until now been done in Europe and Japan, many mineral-exporting countries are eager to do more of the processing themselves. Tin is now mostly smelted in the countries where it is mined; steel production has grown rapidly in Brazil, India and other third-world countries that produce iron ore; Chile and Zambia refine more copper than any European country. Aluminium, however, is made by processes that require huge supplies of electricity; the smelters are sited near energy sources, rather than near bauxite mines, and for this reason Canada and Norway rank high among the producing countries.

Much mineral wealth lies beneath the sea. New technologies have opened up the prospect of valuable minerals being 'mined' from the deep ocean floor, in areas which, even under the new code of sea law (6), will be beyond the limits of coastal states' jurisdiction. In many places the ocean floor is sprinkled with 'nodules' (lumps) that contain cobalt, copper, manganese and nickel. The states that export these minerals (including Canada, Chile, Zaire and Zambia) have naturally sought, in the negotiations about an international regime for sea bed mining, to get limitations imposed so that the market would not be 'flooded' by the potentially enormous haul from the depths.

The new code lay down the principle that the deep sea bed minerals are part of 'the common heritage of mankind', and the proposed international regime has been designed to ensure that they should not all go to the first-comers – the few countries that are already developing the required technology. American objections to some of the more restrictive clauses in this part of the code have been one of the causes of the long delay in ratification (6). These disputes are, however, rather long-term ones. Great changes, either in technology or in the economic setting, will be necessary to make deep sea bed 'mining' a worthwhile venture.

6 Sea law

Seven-tenths of the earth's surface is covered by the 'seven seas'. Until the middle of this century, nearly all this vast area was regarded as the 'high seas', under no national jurisdiction. Maritime countries upheld the principle of freedom of navigation. Most coastal states claimed territorial waters extending only three nautical miles from shore (100 nautical miles are about 115 land miles or 185 km). But sea claims were getting bigger; 12-mile limits became more numerous, and some states proclaimed 200-mile ones. United Nations conferences on the law of the sea (UNCLOS) in 1958 and 1960 failed to resolve the problems. In the 1950s and 1960s Britain, Iceland and Norway were among the states that became embroiled over fishing rights (22). However, the 1958 conference did produce a convention on rights to the oil and gas beneath the relatively shallow waters of 'continental shelf' areas such as the North Sea.

From 1974 to 1982 the third UNCLOS negotiated a whole new code of sea law suited to an age in which disputes over fisheries, offshore oil and freedom of navigation were becoming more numerous and dangerous. In 1982 this code was approved, but the voting was not unanimous, and there were doubts about when or whether the new code would take effect.

It was agreed to authorize 12-mile limits and to allow each coastal state, in addition, a 200-mile 'exclusive economic zone (EEZ), in which it would control both mineral and fishing rights – as well as having mineral rights on the 'shelf' (which varies in width, and in some places extends far more than 200 miles from shore). During the 1970s claims to EEZs were announced by most of the coastal states, which thus 'jumped the gun' by asserting claims based on the new code without waiting for it to come into force.

A third of all the oceans are brought under the jurisdiction of coastal states by the introduction of EEZs. These zones affect the whole of the Caribbean and Mediterranean seas as well as large parts of the oceans. Even a tiny island may be entitled to a sea zone of about 130,000 square miles. Between states that are close neighbours, the division of overlapping EEZ and shelf zones can often be settled by drawing a median line, equidistant from their coasts; but many disputes have arisen over this (e.g. between Greece and Turkey, Libya and Malta, Norway and the USSR, 22,

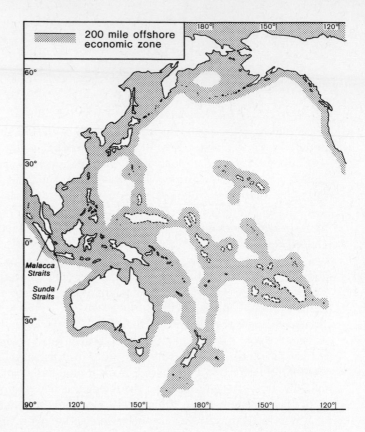

26, 38). Moreover, disputes over small islands may be intensified when claims to large sea areas go with them; this applied to Argentina's long dispute with Chile over the Beagle Channel islets and to its seizure of the Falklands and South Georgia in 1982 (72).

The new code gives coastal states more power to limit marine pollution (e.g. tankers dumping residual oil at sea), but it upholds the general right of free navigation in EEZs. It also upholds freedom of navigation through straits of international importance, even though the approval of 12-mile limits may mean that some of these straits become the territorial waters of the coastal states on each side; the Dover and Gibraltar straits, for example, are respectively only 21 and 9 miles wide at their narrowest points. These principles do not apply to the Suez and Panama canals (41, 70), although they, too, are of great importance to world shipping; they are subject to special rules and agreements, as are the Turkish straits (the

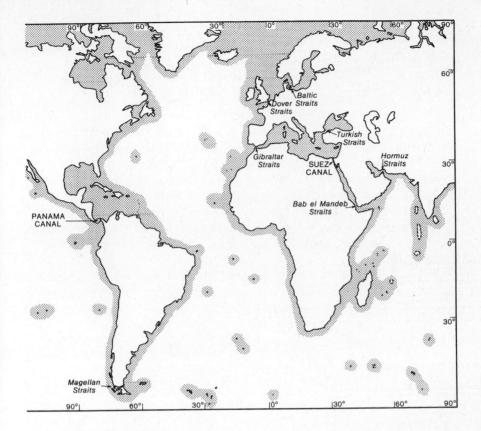

Dardanelles and Bosphorus), where the two coasts belong to the same country.

One of the most complicated parts of the new code of sea law is the proposed international regime intended to regulate deep sea bed 'mining' (5). American opposition made it seem particularly doubtful whether this section of the code would ever come into force without amendment. For the whole code to take effect, 60 ratifications were required; up to 1990 only 42 countries had ratified it. Meanwhile, with regard to EEZs, 12-mile limits and some other points, many governments were behaving as if the code were already in force.

7 Three worlds?

Between the late 1940s and the early 1960s the world's nations seemed to become divided into three groups – often labelled 'east', 'west' and 'south'. The USSR and the east European states which it had brought under its control during and after the 1939–45 war (*13, 16*) sealed themselves off behind their 'iron curtain', and the civil war in China added it, too, to the communist 'eastern bloc'. Fear of Soviet armed strength led most of the democratic European states to seek close links with the USA and Canada (*20*); a few remained 'neutral', but the basic 'east–west' division became very clear.

Between them, these two camps held most of the world's economic power and most of its modern armaments (*2, 10*), and there were global repercussions each time they collided over such east–west issues as Berlin,

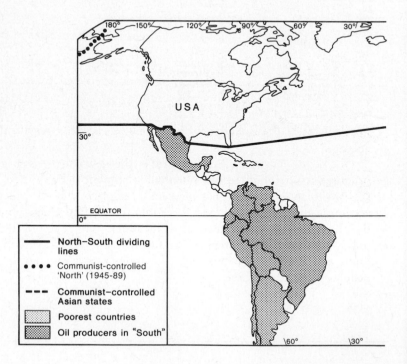

Cuba or Korea (*18, 58, 69*). But the third-world states of Asia, Africa and Latin America, many of which emerged from European colonial rule in this period (*27*), were less interested in east–west issues than in north–south ones.

East, west, south and north are obviously not accurate terms as used here. Australia and New Zealand have usually been included with the states labelled 'north'; Japan, often, with those labelled 'west'. Is China east, or south, or both? The south may be mainly 'non-white' and poorer than the mainly 'white' and richer 'north'; in official jargon, the north may be called 'developed' and the south 'developing'; but the south, in reality, includes some countries that are not developing at all, and others that are richer than many northern ones.

By the 1980s more than 100 third-world governments had joined the 'non-aligned' movement, which had been founded in 1961 at a conference held in Belgrade but mainly representing Asian and African states. They pressed for completion of the decolonizing process (*9, 27, 30*); for more generous terms of trade and aid from the 'north'; and, in principle, for east–west *détente*.

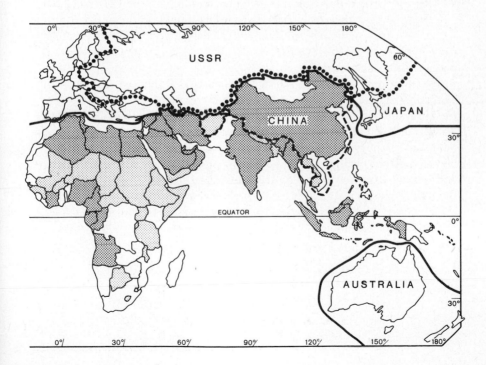

27

The theories behind that last point were that the world would become a safer place and also that the northern powers would switch funds from their arms race to development aid. In practice, many southern governments had exploited the east–west rift, playing one side against the other profitably. In 1990, when they saw the major powers working together through the United Nations on some issues, their diplomats at the UN spoke of the 'frightening' prospect of those powers jointly imposing a 'dictatorship'. The south also foresaw much western aid being allotted to eastern Europe and the USSR.

The simple 'three worlds' line-up had become less simple long before 1990. Many 'non-aligned' states were in fact inclining towards the west, or towards the USSR, or towards China – whose break with the USSR in the 1960s had split the 'eastern' camp. In the 1970s the *rapprochement* between China and the United States changed the picture, and the 'oil shocks' widened the gulf between OPEC's new-rich members and the south's poorest oil-importing states (*3, 40*). By the early 1980s some third-world countries were deep in debt, while the Asian 'little dragons' (*54*) and others were reaching western levels of income per head.

After 1985, with a new Soviet leadership wooing both the US and China (*2, 13, 15, 53*), it became easier to end or mitigate some conflicts in the third world – e.g. in Angola, Afghanistan, Nicaragua (*34, 49, 69*). Unfortunately, the ending of the Iran–Iraq war freed Iraq's ruler to pounce on Kuwait, precipitating a new crisis (*45, 48*).

However, both at the end of Iraq's Iran war and at the start of its Kuwait war, the 'first' and 'second' worlds seemed closer together than ever, while the third world was deeply divided. There were moments in 1990 when the 'three worlds' concept seemed quite dead. Yet some signs pointed the other way. Iraq's ruler could win support for his aggression by whipping up anti-western feeling in some southern countries. And the Soviet rulers, after letting east Europeans go free, answered the pleas for freedom of some nationalities inside the USSR by reverting to old-style tough tactics, complete with tanks. The factors that underlay the original three-way division still had life in them.

8 One world?

In the 1930s there were only 70 sovereign states. Now there are more than 160, mainly because so many former European dependencies have become independent (*27, 65, 71*). World government is still a distant dream, but since 1945 a world organization, the United Nations, has provided its members with means of working together – when they choose – to avert conflicts, or at least to limit their harmful effects.

The UN's original membership was lopsided. It excluded the countries defeated in the 1939–45 war; only a few Asian and African states were then independent; of the 51 founders, 20 were Latin American states; the USSR got two extra seats, normally for its Ukrainian and Byelorussian republics (*14, 15*). By 1990 the membership was 159 – more cumbrous, but more complete, and more balanced in proportion to the populations of the world's main regions. China's seat, long held by the government that ruled only in Taiwan, had passed in 1971 to the government that ruled mainland China (*55*). The remaining non-members were Switzerland, South and North Korea, and a few very small European and Pacific states such as Monaco and Tuvalu. The third-world states (*7*) now have a large majority in the General Assembly, but in the Security Council each of five major powers has a permanent seat and can veto decisions on important questions, on Charter amendments, and on the choice of a new chief for the Secretariat.

Under the UN flag, soldiers from many different countries fought a war to resist aggression in Korea (*58*), and have manned peacekeeping forces and observer groups which have halted or mitigated conflicts in other troubled areas. With varying degrees of success, the UN has been involved in attempts to deal with disputes and conflicts in almost every part of the world. It has seen 11 trust territories achieve independence or merge with neighbouring states. With its 'family' of specialized agencies, it has channelled aid to millions of refugees and to most of the countries of the 'third world'.

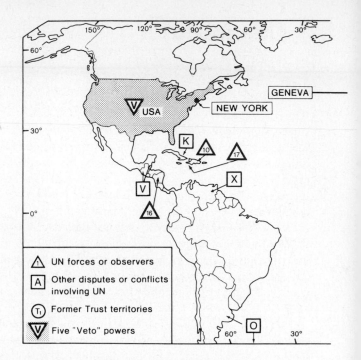

Operations by UN forces or observers

1   Greek frontiers, 1946–9 (*17*)
2   Indonesia, 1947–51 (*63*)
3   Palestine/Israel, Egypt,
    Lebanon, 1947– (*42–4*)
4   Kashmir, 1948– (*50*)
5   Korea, 1950–3 (*58*)
6   Congo/Zaire, 1960–4 (*32*)
7   West Irian, 1962–3 (*63*)
8   Yemen, 1963–4 (*45*)
9   Cyprus, 1964– (*26*)
10 Dominican Republic, 1965 (*69*)
11 India–Pakistan, 1965 (*51*)
12 Iran–Iraq, 1988– (*48*)
13 Afghanistan, 1989– (*49*)
14 Angola, 1989– (*34*)
15 Namibia, 1989–90 (*34*)
16 Central America, 1989– (*69*)
17 Haiti, 1990 (*69*)

Former UN trust territories

T1 Togolands (*36*)
T2 Cameroons (*36*)
T3 Rwanda, Burundi (*35*)
T4 Tanganyika (*35*)
T5 Somalia (*35*)
T6 North-east New Guinea (*63*)
T7 Nauru (*65*)
T8 Western Samoa (*65*)

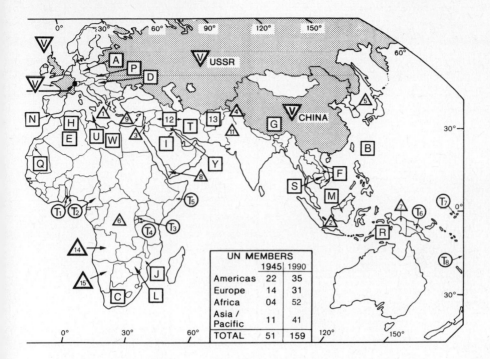

Other disputes and conflicts involving the UN

A   West Berlin, 1948–9 (*18*)
B   Taiwan, 1949–71 (*55*)
C   South Africa, 1952– (*33*)
D   Hungary, 1956 (*16*)
E   Algeria, 1956–61 (*38*)
F   Indochina, 1958–66 (*60*)
G   Tibet, 1959–61 (*52*)
H   Tunisia, 1961 (*38*)
I   Kuwait, 1961–3 (*46*)
J   Mozambique, etc., 1961–75 (*31*)
K   Cuba, 1962 (*69*)
L   Rhodesia/Zimbabwe, 1962–79 (*32*)

M   Borneo, 1963–5 (*62*)
N   Gibraltar, 1965– (*25*)
O   Falklands, 1965– (*72*)
P   Czechoslovakia, 1968 (*16*)
Q   Western Sahara, 1974– (*39*)
R   East Timor, 1975– (*63*)
S   Cambodia, 1979– (*61*)
T   Iran–USA, 1979–80 (*47*)
U   Malta–Libya, 1980 (*38*)
V   Belize–Guatemala, 1981 (*69*)
W   Libya–USA, 1986 (*38*)
X   Venezuela–Guyana, 1986–7 (*71*)
Y   Iraq–Kuwait, 1990– (*45*)

9 Commonwealth

The Commonwealth is a voluntary association of states which were once parts of the British empire. The old Dominions were confirmed in their independence by the 1931 Statute of Westminster; India and Pakistan became independent in 1947; the 'decolonization' of the rest of the empire followed, and by 1965 there were 22 sovereign Commonwealth member states; by 1975, 35 of them; and by 1990, 50.

The former Irish Free State (*24*) left the Commonwealth on becoming a republic in 1949. South Africa (*33*) left in 1961. Pakistan withdrew in 1972 (when Bangladesh, formerly East Pakistan, was admitted) but returned in 1989 (*51*); entry or re-entry depends on acceptance by the other members, and India had blocked Pakistan's re-entry for some time. The membership of Fiji (*65*) was suspended in 1987.

Membership was not contemplated for some states which had not been formally classed as British dependencies, although they had been under British control for a time – e.g. Bahrain or Sudan (*35, 46*). On the other hand, Vanuatu, a former British–French condominium, joined in 1980 and Namibia, formerly ruled by South Africa, in 1990 (*34, 65*).

Two very small states, Nauru and Tuvalu (*65*), are 'special members'; they take part in many activities, but not in the meetings of heads of government (prime ministers and presidents) that are normally held every

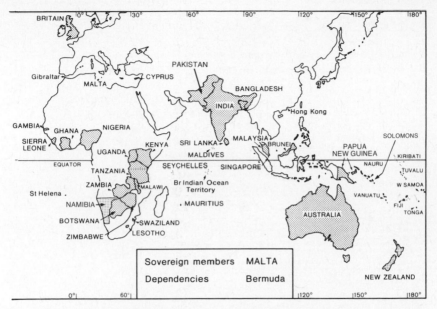

Sovereign members MALTA

Dependencies Bermuda

second year. The smaller and poorer member states have, as a rule, bene-
fited most from the services of the Secretariat, the technical co-operation
fund and other joint institutions, but all members have found the association advantageous, and even some of the states that have withdrawn have
retained some advantages of membership.

The member governments have often disagreed – for example, over
how much economic pressure to apply to South Africa (*33*). But predictions that Britain's entry into the European Community (*19*) would destroy
the Commonwealth proved wrong. With its expansion, the Commonwealth had become a bridge between nations with many different interests
and viewpoints; with its flexibility, states had found that they could belong
to it and also to regional groups or even to alliances.

Commonwealth states are listed here by continents, with dates of admission (except for the oldest members). Republics, and states that have their
own separate monarchies, are indicated by *r* or *o* respectively. In each of
the remaining countries the head of state is Queen Elizabeth II (whom all
members also acknowledge as Head of the Commonwealth). She is represented, in each of these states (except Britain), by a governor-general,
whose appointment is a matter for that country alone; the title is the only
vestige of the former imperial authority.

Europe	Africa	Asia
Britain	r Botswana, 1966	r Bangladesh, 1972
r Cyprus, 1961	r Gambia, 1965	o Brunei, 1984
r Malta, 1964	r Ghana, 1957	r India, 1947
	r Kenya, 1963	o Malaysia, 1957
Americas	o Lesotho, 1966	r Maldives, 1982
	r Malawi, 1964	r Pakistan, 1947
Antigua, 1981	Mauritius, 1968	r Singapore, 1965
Bahamas, 1973	r Namibia, 1990	r Sri Lanka, 1948
Barbados, 1966	r Nigeria, 1960	
Belize, 1981	r Seychelles, 1976	Pacific
Canada	r Sierra Leone, 1961	
r Dominica, 1978	o Swaziland, 1968	Australia
Grenada, 1974	r Tanzania, 1961	(Fiji) 1970
r Guyana, 1966	r Uganda, 1962	r Kiribati, 1979
Jamaica, 1962	r Zambia, 1964	r Nauru, 1968
St Kitts, 1983	r Zimbabwe, 1980	New Zealand
St Lucia, 1979		Papua New Guinea,
St Vincent, 1979		1975
r Trinidad, 1962		Solomons, 1978
		o Tonga, 1970
		r Tuvalu, 1978
		r Vanuatu, 1980
		r Western Samoa, 1962

10 The long arm of war

In 1945 the American atomic bombs dropped on Hiroshima and Nagasaki brought the Japanese war to a swift end, and may well have saved far more lives than they took. But, ever since, the destructive power of nuclear weapons has caused widespread horror and fear, and the great increase in that power has aroused fears that a full-scale nuclear war might destroy mankind. World affairs have been influenced by these weapons' mere existence; by their being brandished as a threat, or as a deterrent to the use of 'conventional' force; by some states' attempts to acquire them, and by others' efforts to curb their proliferation (4). The Soviet attempt to place nuclear missiles in Cuba in 1962 set off one of the post-1945 period's most acute international crises (69).

China joined the USA, the USSR, Britain and France as the fifth nuclear-armed power when it staged its first test explosion in 1964. India

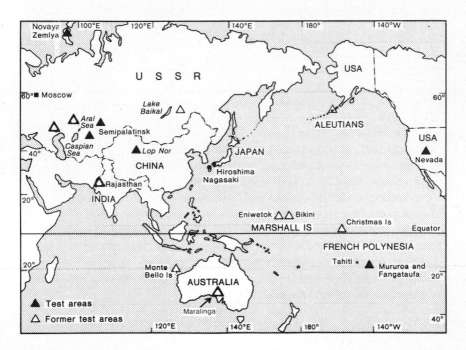

35

set off a nuclear explosion in 1974, but claimed that its purpose was non-military. No other countries have staged identifiable tests. As to 'the Five', three of them – Britain, USA, USSR – promised, in the 1963 'partial test ban' treaty, to stage their tests only in underground cavities, so that they would not send masses of radioactive debris into the atmosphere. France limited itself to underground tests from 1974 on, and China from 1980.

Meanwhile nuclear strategy had been transformed. The USA and USSR had built intercontinental ballistic missiles (ICBMs) with ranges of well over 6,000 miles. In the 1980s each superpower's ICBMs were capable of delivering several thousand warheads on to the other's territory. Each was keeping at sea submarines that could hit the other power with nuclear missiles. Britain and France were operating smaller numbers of missile-firing submarines. China had begun to deploy ICBMs.

In the 1970s the USSR started to deploy hundreds of mobile inter-mediate-range missiles (SS–20s) aimed at western Europe. The NATO allies (20) agreed to start deploying new American 'cruise' and other missiles in Europe if the Soviet array of SS–20s was not removed or reduced. The USSR continued to deploy its SS–20s, and the NATO deployment began in 1983, despite much opposition from 'anti-nuclear' groups. However, a new Soviet leadership took over in Moscow in 1985; US–Soviet relations began to improve, and in 1987 the two superpowers concluded a treaty for the elimination of intermediate-range nuclear forces (INF); 2,600 missiles were to be destroyed, including the Soviet SS–20s and the NATO ones intended to counter them. The prospects for further disarmament deals looked good. In 1990 a treaty on reduction of conventional forces in Europe (CFE) was signed in Paris by the 16 NATO governments and the six remaining Warsaw Pact ones (13), just after the unification of Germany (18). The CFE treaty provided for phased reductions, spread over 40 months after ratification of the treaty by all 22 signatories, which would leave the two alliances with forces of roughly equal size in the area between the Ural mountains and the Atlantic.

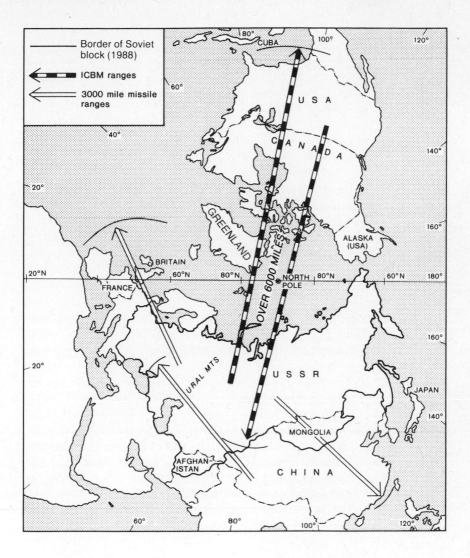

Border of Soviet block (1988)

ICBM ranges

3000 mile missile ranges

OVER 6000 MILES

USA

CANADA

GREENLAND

ALASKA (USA)

BRITAIN

FRANCE

NORTH POLE

URAL MTS

USSR

JAPAN

MONGOLIA

AFGHAN-ISTAN

CHINA

80°   100°   120°

60°

40°

20°

20°N   60°N   80°N   80°N   60°N   180°

20°

20°

60°   80°   100°   120°

140°

160°

160°

140°

11 Arctic

The first man at (or near) the North Pole was Robert Peary, who got there in 1909, using dog-drawn sledges. By 1958 other Americans could pass under the Pole in a nuclear-powered submarine which travelled beneath the ice from Pacific to Atlantic. By then, too, airliners were crossing the Arctic on regular flights between Europe and Japan by way of Alaska. Things have moved fast in the far north. The USSR has staged nuclear-bomb tests in Novaya Zemlya (*10*), including, in 1961, the biggest man-made explosion yet recorded. There are coal mines in Svalbard (Spitsbergen, *22*) and huge oilfields near Prudhoe Bay on the North Slope in Alaska (*67*); oil and gas have also been found among Canada's Arctic islands (*68*).

Political change has come to the region. Alaska became the forty-ninth state of the USA in 1959. Iceland's constitutional links with Denmark ended when it became an independent republic in 1944. Greenland, a former Danish dependency given country status in 1953, obtained 'home rule' in 1979 (*21*).

In the early 1980s there was controversy over the plans to pipe more Soviet gas to western Europe from fields near the Ob river estuary in north-western Siberia. In the Soviet Arctic, development had long been linked with the large-scale use of prisoners as a labour force, from the coal mines around Vorkuta to the gold mines of the Kolyma region. Whole districts were run by the KGB as gigantic 'gulags' (*15*).

On the map the stippled areas show the difference between maximum and minimum (that is, midwinter and midsummer) ice coverage of the northern seas (*22*). This is particularly significant for the USSR. Ships equipped for icebreaking can reach ports all along the Siberian coast each summer season (and great efforts have been made to lengthen the 'open season'). But only around Murmansk, near the Norwegian frontier, is there a truly ice-free stretch of Soviet coast from which warships and nuclear missile-firing submarines can enter the Atlantic without having to pass through straits in the Baltic or the Mediterranean.

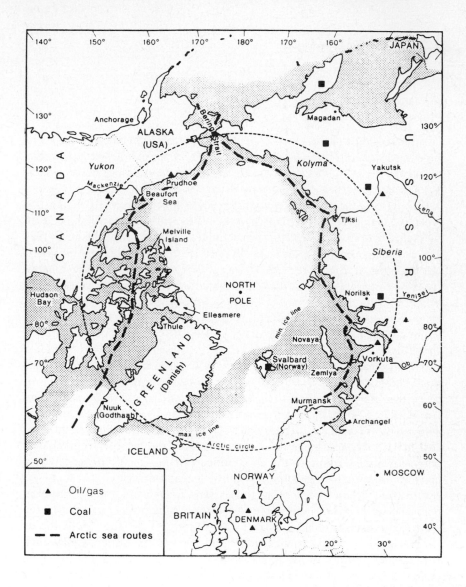

140° 150° 160° 170° 180° 170° 160° JAPAN

130° Anchorage Bering Strait Magadan

ALASKA (USA)

120° Yukon Kolyma Yakutsk

Mackenzie Prudhoe Lena

110° Beaufort Sea Tiksi

100° Melville Island Siberia 100°

Hudson Bay NORTH POLE Norilsk Yenisei

80° Ellesmere min ice line 80°

Thule Novaya Ob

70° GREENLAND (Danish) Svalbard (Norway) Zemlya Vorkuta 70°

Nuuk (Godthaab) Murmansk 60°

max ice line Archangel

50° ICELAND Arctic circle 50°

NORWAY MOSCOW

▲ Oil/gas

■ Coal

BRITAIN DENMARK 40°

▬ ▬ Arctic sea routes

0° 20° 30°

CANADA

U S S R

12 Antarctic

Claims to sectors of the Antarctic continent's 5.5 million square miles have been made by Australia, Britain, France, New Zealand and Norway, which recognize each other's claims, and by Argentina and Chile, whose claims overlap Britain's and each other's. In 1959 these seven nations, together with Belgium, Japan, South Africa, the USA and the USSR, signed the Antarctic Treaty. Other nations later acceded to the treaty; by 1990 14 of them had mounted enough research activity to qualify for full voting rights alongside the original 12 'consultative parties'. The treaty banned military activity, the dumping of nuclear waste (4) and new territorial claims (parties were not committed to recognizing any existing claims). All research bases were to be open to inspection, so that any violation of the treaty could be exposed. (The Greenpeace organization said in 1990 that its teams had visited 35 bases and found alarming signs of pollution at several of them.)

The treaty applied to the area south of latitude 60° South. In 1980 the treaty states signed a convention on conservation of marine living resources which applied to the larger area encircled by the Antarctic Convergence – the line where warmer water overlays the near-freezing Antarctic surface water. (These waters contain huge amounts of shrimp-like krill, harvested by Soviet, Japanese and other trawlers.) The 1980 convention came into effect in 1982. In 1988 the treaty states signed a convention on the regulation of mineral resource activities. By 1990, however, it seemed clear that some signatories would not ratify this convention. Environmentalist groups were pressing for a complete ban on mining and drilling for oil.

Antarctica has no permanent population – only the scientists manning the research stations or bases. It was the British Antarctic Survey team at Halley base who discovered, in 1982, the hole in the earth's protective ozone layer, above the Antarctic, that man-made chlorofluorocarbons (CFCs) had made (1). In 1990 there were fears that a similar hole might appear above the Arctic.

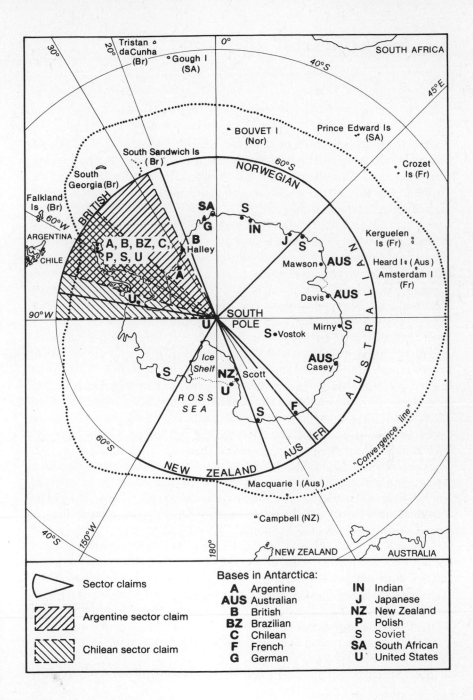

13 Europe: east and west

In the two years 1989 and 1990 the face of Europe was changed. This was the end of a 45-year period during which the continent had been more sharply divided into two parts than ever before (except in wartime). The division was not merely political but human: eastern Europe's rulers barred its inhabitants from free contact with their western neighbours, tightly restricting both travel and the exchange of information.

In 1944–5, when Nazi Germany's hold on Europe was broken (*18*), the advancing Soviet army imposed Soviet control on Poland, Hungary, Rumania, Bulgaria, East Germany and, until 1955, part of Austria. Communist regimes, then closely linked with the USSR, were also established in Jugoslavia and Albania. An 'iron curtain of silence' (in Winston Churchill's words) fell across the middle of Europe. Two gaps in the 'curtain' remained: West Berlin, surrounded by Soviet-held territory but garrisoned by American, British and French troops (*18*), and Czechoslovakia, where communist rule was not imposed so quickly as in other east European countries. But in 1948 a Soviet-backed communist coup turned Czechoslovakia into one more police state, and the USSR also blockaded West Berlin in an attempt to break its fragile links with the west. In the same year, however, Jugoslavia's communist rulers broke away from the Soviet bloc (*17*).

The USSR made formal alliances with its east European 'satellite' states, whose armed forces were, in practice, already under Soviet control; in 1955 these alliances were consolidated as the Warsaw Pact. The Soviet economic grip on the satellites was formalized by the creation in 1949 of the Council for Mutual Economic Aid (CMEA, more often called Comecon). Albania withdrew from both Pact and Comecon when it quarrelled with the USSR in the 1960s; it could do so safely, because Jugoslavia, although hostile to it, shielded it geographically. Hungary and Czechoslovakia had no such shield, and their bids for liberation (*16*) were crushed by the Soviet army. (East Germany, Poland, Hungary and Bulgaria were compelled to send troops to help subdue Czechoslovakia in 1968; this shed a revealing light on the difference between the Warsaw Pact and any genuine alliance.)

The Soviet rulers repeatedly called for east–west European 'security'

talks and agreements; their main aim was to legitimize the partition of Germany and the communist domination of eastern Europe, but what eventually emerged suited them less well. In 1975, after long negotiations in the Conference on Security and Co-operation in Europe (CSCE), an agreement as signed at Helsinki by the United States and Canada (whose participation had been reluctantly accepted by the USSR) as well as by 33 European governments – Albania being the one absentee. The Helsinki text included promises that all signatories, including the USSR, would promote freedom of movement and contact between their countries. The Soviet bloc's regimes flouted these promises, and persecuted the 'Helsinki groups' that asked them to comply. But most of the western governments continued to call for compliance, especially at CSCE review conferences held in Belgrade and Madrid between 1977 and 1983.

The 'iron curtain' remained, with minefields along frontiers, the jamming of western broadcasts, and all the other complex and costly things that prevented Europeans from achievng the security and co-operation that were the CSCE's proclaimed goals. But the Helsinki idea spread among the peoples of eastern Europe. A third CSCE review conference, held in Vienna, dragged on from 1986 to early 1989 because of Soviet reluctance to ease any restrictions but then at last brought some Soviet concessions. The 'curtain' was still merely swaying. Then the pace quickened, and it began to collapse.

Poland and Hungary led the way. Poland was first to install a non-communist government. Hungary allowed thousands of East Germans to pass through it to the west. Mass protests in East Germany forced its rulers to breach the Berlin wall (*18*) and open the border with West Germany before the end of 1989; by the end of 1990 East Germany no longer existed. By then Czechoslovakia, Hungary and Poland had all elected non-communist governments; in Bulgaria and Rumania the old communist bosses had gone and other communists, who had changed their labels and methods, were struggling to retain power (*16*). Jugoslavia seemed close to a new balkanization, with its western components, under non-communist leadership, breaking away from Serbia; even Albania's rulers were having to fake a 'multi-party' system (*17*).

The USSR, which was itself in danger of breaking up, had done nothing to save its old clients in the east European regimes; but it had no great wish to help eastern Europe's new governments. It reduced oil deliveries, sharply raised the price of the oil it did deliver, and stripped bare the installations that its withdrawing troops vacated. West Europeans, particularly Germans, faced new questions about the best means, and the cost, of helping eastern Europe to undo the damage done by economic mismanagement based on Marxist dogmas (urban pollution and rural poverty being two conspicuous problems). The view through the new 'windows' that had replaced the iron curtain was not pleasant. But at least Europeans could now see Europe as more of a whole than most of them had ever known it to be.

In non-communist western Europe, by 1989, the North Atlantic Treaty (NATO) alliance had 16 members, although France had withdrawn its forces from the NATO command structure (*20*). For various reasons, Austria, Finland, Ireland, Sweden and Switzerland had remained 'neutral'. They were, however, visibly on the western side of the iron curtain; until

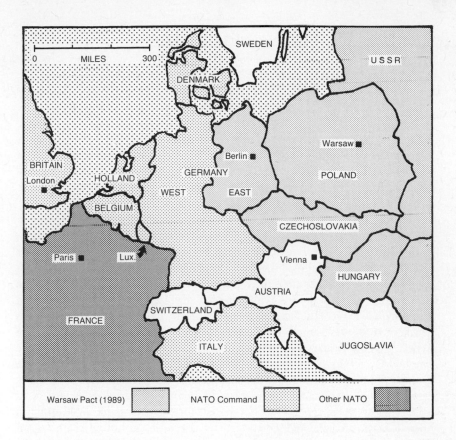

1989, Austria's communist neighbours kept their frontiers with it tightly sealed (*18*) – nor did they allow their inhabitants to escape to the west by way of communist but 'non-aligned' Jugoslavia (*17*).

14 Soviet territorial gains

In 1989–90 the world was suddenly reminded of the scale of the USSR's acquisition of territory during and after the 1939–45 war. Estonia, Latvia and Lithuania, the three 'Baltic states', which it had annexed in 1940, came back into the international spotlight when they pressed claims for the restoration of their independence, after nearly 50 years.

The Baltic states, however, represented less than half of the 200,000 square miles of European territory gained by the Soviet Union in 1939–45 – gains which gave it a long Baltic coastline and brought it to the mouth of the Danube (16, 21). In 1939 the USSR occupied eastern Poland (thousands of Poles were carried off to their death in camps such as those in Katyn forest, near Smolensk – a crime at last admitted in 1990) and invaded Finland (the Finns, like the Poles and the Balts, had freed themselves from Russia's rule after its 1917 revolutions). In 1940, as well as occupying the Baltic states, it forced Rumania to cede Bessarabia (most of which became the USSR's Moldavian republic) and part of Bukovina. In 1944 it made the Finns cede part of Karelia for the second time (21) and took more territory from them, including Petsamo (now Pechenga), their only Arctic port. Retaining all these gains after 1945, it also took Transcarpathia (Ruthenia) from Czechoslovakia and northern East Prussia, including Kaliningrad (formerly Königsberg), from Germany. Altogether, the Soviet rulers gained 25 million more subjects.

The land taken from Poland and Czechoslovakia was incorporated in the USSR's Ukrainian and Byelorussian republics. (In 1990 it was in the western Ukraine, around Lvov, that calls for Ukrainian independence were loudest.) The Kaliningrad region became a detached part of the Russian republic; its German inhabitants were expelled, and it was largely repopulated with Russian soldiers and their families. Many Russians were settled in the three Baltic republics (replacing deported Balts). By the 1980s, Russian-speakers made up 40% of Estonia's population, 45–50% of Latvia's and 15% of Lithuania's.

One victim of the Soviet annexations, Poland, was 'compensated' by being given areas taken from Germany; in effect, Poland was bodily shifted westwards, to a frontier on the rivers Oder and Neisse (18).

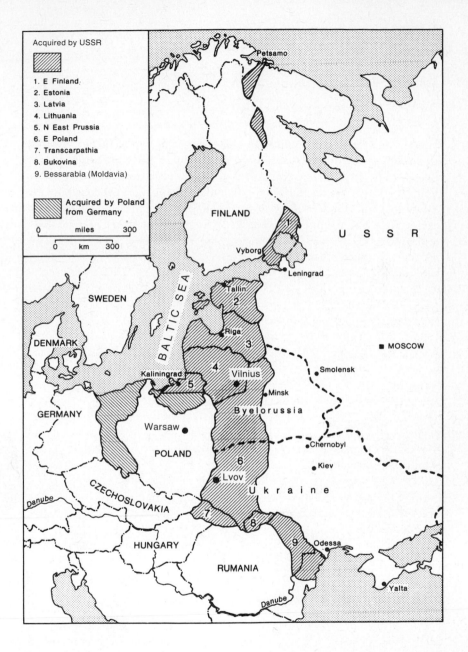

Acquired by USSR

1. E Finland
2. Estonia
3. Latvia
4. Lithuania
5. N East Prussia
6. E Poland
7. Transcarpathia
8. Bukovina
9. Bessarabia (Moldavia)

Acquired by Poland
from Germany

miles 0 — 300
km 0 — 300

Petsamo

FINLAND

U S S R

SWEDEN

BALTIC SEA

Vyborg

Leningrad

Tallin

2

Riga

3

MOSCOW

DENMARK

Smolensk

Kaliningrad

4

Vilnius

5

Minsk

GERMANY

B y e l o r u s s i a

Warsaw

Chernobyl

POLAND

6

Kiev

CZECHOSLOVAKIA

Lvov

U k r a i n e

Danube

7

8

HUNGARY

9

Odessa

RUMANIA

Danube

Yalta

15 Soviet Union (USSR)

The Union of Soviet Socialist Republics never was that. In 1990 its own president, Mikhail Gorbachov, admitted that it had 'pretended to be federal while in fact it was unitary'. In practice, it had been even more tightly controlled from the centre than was its pre-1917 predecessor, the tsarist Russian empire. But, on paper, it was a federation of 15 union

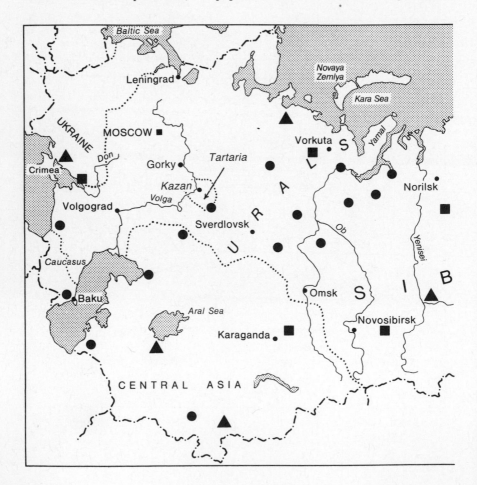

republics, one for each of the main national groups; the Russian one (RSFSR) being the biggest, and itself containing 16 'autonomous republics' (ASSRs) of smaller nationalities (e.g. Buryat–Mongol, Tartar, Yakut) and 15 still smaller 'autonomous' regions and areas.

In 1990 most of the union republics and many of the smaller entities were demanding to be allowed in practice rights which they already had on paper – including the right to leave the USSR; in theory, each union republic had always been free to secede. The three Baltic republics (*14*) said they repudiated their annexation by the USSR in 1940, as it had been illegal. There were stirrings even in the Ukraine, especially in the western region around Lvov, which the USSR had seized in 1939 when it joined

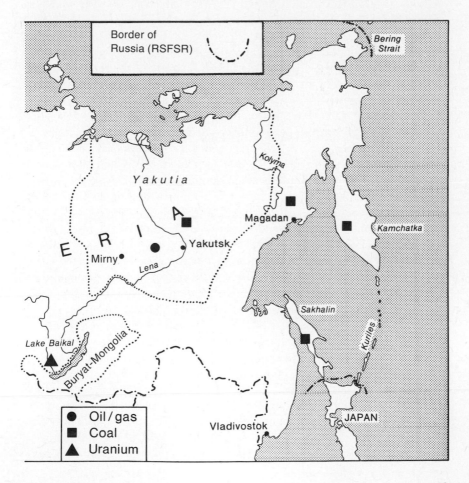

Nazi Germany in partitioning Poland (*14, 18*). (Ukrainians and Byelorussians are Slavs of much the same stock as Russians, but long association with Poland and Lithuania has left them with distinctive languages and traditions.)

This nationalist turbulence, long simmering beneath the surface, had come into the open when Gorbachov, recognizing the stifling effect of the Soviet monopolistic system, allowed the republics, for the first time, to hold elections in which the communists could be challenged. Wherever the voting was really free, nationalist parties won. Within six months after the elections held in early 1990, four republics had declared independence and 13 had proclaimed that their laws overrode Soviet ones. The Russian republic was openly challenging the Soviet government with which it shared the capital, Moscow.

Russians make up almost half of the USSR's population, Ukrainians and Byelorussians another fifth, non-Slav peoples the remainder. Taking the Ural mountains as the dividing line, three-quarters of the total area is in Asia but two-thirds of the population is in Europe, much of Siberia being very thinly peopled; in central Asia, however, although there are large deserts (including recently man-made ones around the Aral Sea, *1*), the Muslim peoples' rate of population growth is now strikingly high, at around 3% per year (*1, 28, 53*). Siberia's natural resources have enabled the USSR to become the world's biggest producer of oil and the second biggest producer of gold and gem diamonds (*3, 5*). Much of the labour force used to exploit these resources has been provided by the network of prison camp complexes – the 'Gulag Archipelago' – among which the 'gulags' around Karaganda and Vorkuta and along the Kolyma have earned a special notoriety (*11*). During Stalin's reign more than 33 million people were sent to the camps, and about 18 million died there; in the 1980s gulag labour helped to build the BAM railway (*53*) and the gas pipelines from new fields around the Ob estuary to eastern and western Europe (*3*).

Pre-1917 Russia was a major exporter of grain and had Europe's fastest-growing economy. In 1989 the USSR had to import 33 million tons of grain, and total output and living standards were both falling. When Gorbachov came to the top of the old communist hierarchy, he called for economic reforms; but the hierarchy, clutching at its privileges, obstructed them so systematically that conditions actually deteriorated. The failure of the centralized system, and the failure to change it, encouraged separatism.

In the central Asian republics (*53*) there were ethnic conflicts – e.g. between Uzbeks and Kirghiz – in 1990, but in general the communists, backed by troops, kept control. The Caucasus was more chaotic. A pro-

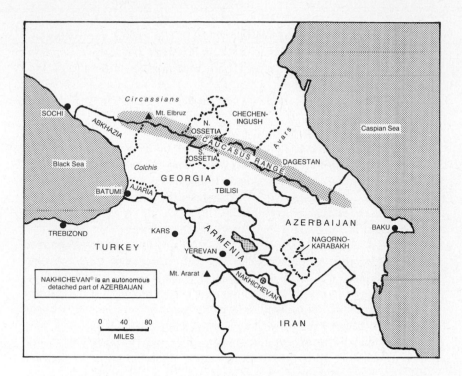

independence government in Georgia, which feared that the Soviet army
would march in and oust it, also faced separatist break-aways by Abkhazia
and South Ossetia. Muslim Azerbaijan and Christian Armenia were virtually at war with one another (while both were rejecting orders from
Moscow); 600,000 people had fled from the two republics since they
started to fight over Nagorno-Karabakh, an Armenian-peopled district in
Azerbaijan. The Azeris of Azerbaijan were restoring links with their kinsfolk in Iran (47). Across the Black Sea, the Moldavians were demanding
the right to be reunited with Rumania's Moldavians (14, 16).

The three Baltic republics (14) seemed at the end of 1990 to be on a
collision course with a Gorbachov who, by then, had lost his more liberal
associates. Many people feared that he would yield to the obvious eager-
ness of the KGB (political police) and the other armed forces to crush the
Lithuanian, Latvian and Estonian independence movements – which
included many members of the Russian-speaking minorities in the region.

16 Eastern Europe

The transformation of eastern Europe in 1989–90 was one of the most momentous events of the late twentieth century. The key factor was that the USSR would no longer use its military power to pin the region down under the communist regimes which that military power had originally imposed, and later reimposed. What had been called 'a chain of fear stretching back to Moscow' was broken.

At the 1945 conference at Yalta, in the Crimea, the USSR had agreed with the USA and Britain that the nations liberated from the Nazi German empire (*18*) should be enabled to 'create democratic institutions of their own choice'. It then violated the Yalta agreement ruthlessly. Rigged elections were held, and communist governments installed; democratic leaders were jailed, and many were killed; although some non-communist political parties were ostensibly allowed to survive, they were all 'purged' and turned into docile groups of 'fellow-travellers' (*13*). In Jugoslavia and Albania, which the Soviet army did not occupy, similar regimes were set up by their own communists (*17*).

Austria, where democracy had been restored, accepted a commitment to neutrality in 1955 (*18*). The USSR then withdrew its troops from Austria (enabling the western powers to do the same) and urged Germany to follow the 'Austrian example'. But the Soviet propaganda about neutraliity caused stirrings in eastern Europe. The Hungarians, seeing a neutral Austria to the west and, to the south, a neutral Jugoslavia which was then being wooed by the Soviet rulers (*17*), tried to break loose; they installed a coalition government which proposed that Hungary should become neutral. A large Soviet army was sent in, which crushed the Hungarian revolution while much of the world's attention was focused on the 1956 Suez conflict (*42*).

In Czechoslovakia, in the 1960s, the regime's brutality repelled many of the communists themselves; new leaders sought to give it 'a human face' but assured the USSR that they would not turn neutral. The Soviet rulers would not permit even modest reforms; in 1968 another Soviet invasion was launched, the reformers were jailed and a new puppet government was imposed.

In Poland the 1970s brought outbreaks of mass protest – against the

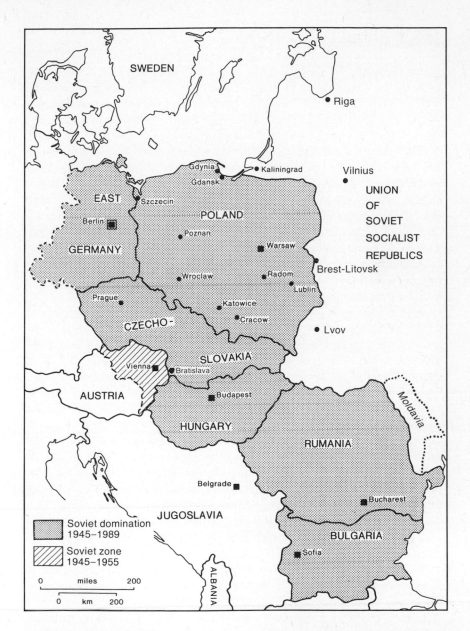

regime's economic mismanagement as well as its inhumanity. A wave of strikes in 1980 forced the regime to let the workers form a free trade union organization, Solidarity. But, when the trade unions went on demanding reforms, the Polish army (which, like other east European armies, was ulti-mately under Soviet control) took over, driving strikers back to work under threat of death. Resistance to the coup was eventually broken even in Gdansk, the shipbuilding port where Solidarity had won its first foothold. The army chief, General Jaruzelski, became head of both government and communist party; Lech Walesa and other Solidarity leaders were locked up.

The Bulgarian and East German (*18*) regimes dutifully toed the Soviet line from the 1940s to the 1980s. Rumania's did not always do so. In 1968 it, alone, refused to send troops to help subdue Czechoslovakia (*13*). But it was as cruelly repressive as any. After the crushing of Hungary in 1956, Rumania clamped down hard on its own Hungarian minority, formally abolishing their 'autonomous' territory in Transylvania, and deporting thousands to the Dobruja swamplands. In the 1980s, when the 2.5 million Hungarians faced new discriminatory measures, as well as the miseries that were inflicted on the whole population of Rumania, thousands escaped into Hungary.

Bulgaria took drastic action against its 1.5 million Muslims, mostly of Turkish origin. In 1984–5 the use of Turkish dress or language was banned, mosques were closed, and people with Turkish-style personal names were given Slav ones. The forcible name-changing had already, in 1972–3, been imposed on the 300,000 Pomaks (Muslims of Slav origin); in both these drives, many people died when troops opened fire if a village tried to resist. In mid-1989 about 325,000 Muslims were driven from their homes and forced to flee into Turkey.

By 1988 Poland's regime could see that its economic problems were too much for it. Early in 1989 it was obliged to negotiate with Solidarity again. In a semi-free election in June, Solidarity won nearly all the seats filled by free voting; in September it formed a government, with Jaruzelski retaining the presidency (until 1990, when Walesa was elected to succeed him).

The ice had cracked. In November the Berlin Wall was opened (*18*). By June 1990 non-communist governments had taken over, after free elec-tions, in East Germany (which ceased to exist in October), Czechoslovakia and Hungary. In Bulgaria, however, the communists hung on. They deposed their old leader in November 1989; they promised to mend their ways, renamed themselves socialists, and won the 1990 election.

Rumania's ruling Ceausescu family, thuggish to the end, went down in bloodshed in December 1989, but many self-styled 'ex-communists' swarmed into the National Salvation Front, which, claiming credit for the 1989 'revolution', won the 1990 election. It then cast doubt on its commit-

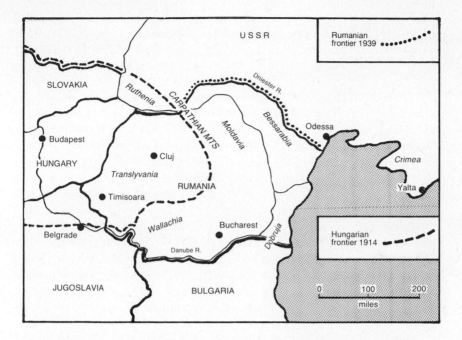

ment to democracy by the violence of its reaction to calls for reform.

Meanwhile, Rumanians' sympathies were engaged by the struggles of their kinsfolk in Bessarabia – the USSR's Moldavian republic (*14*). Other linguistic and ethnic issues were re-emerging as eastern Europe lost its Soviet-imposed facade of unity: Hungary's concern for the Hungarians in Jugoslavia, as well as for those in Rumania; Slovak demands for more autonomy, symbolized by debates about Czechoslovakia being spelt Czecho-Slovakia. In Warsaw, in 1990, the Gypsies' world congress was, for the first time, held in eastern Europe, the region where three-quarters of the world's 10 million Gypsies live.

The new Soviet 'hands off' policy held good through all the 1990 changes, but the east Europeans were still uncertain how far they could go – e.g. in offering support to secessionists in the USSR's Baltic republics (*15*). There were still 500,000 Soviet soldiers in East Germany, Poland, Hungary and Czechoslovakia.

17 Jugoslavia and Albania

After the 1939–45 war, communist regimes took power in Jugoslavia and Albania. Neither country was occupied by Soviet troops, but for a time both followed the Soviet line. Jugoslavia had a quarrel of its own with the western powers, over Trieste. Under the 1947 Italian peace treaty Jugoslavia gained areas north and south of Trieste, but not the city itself, whose population is mainly Italian (and which, in 1945, was captured from the retreating Germans by New Zealand troops). A British and American garrison held Trieste until 1954, when Jugoslavia at last agreed that the city should remain part of Italy. (In 1990 Trieste again attracted international interest. Before 1914 it had been the Austrian empire's great seaport; now the 'pentagonal' talks held between Austria, Czechoslovakia, Hungary, Italy and Jugoslavia revived hopes of restoring its direct rail links with Vienna and Prague.)

In 1948 Jugoslavia's communist rulers broke their ties with the USSR. This rift disrupted the joint Albanian–Jugoslav–Bulgarian support of communist rebels in northern Greece, and in 1949 the last of these rebel forces withdrew into Bulgaria (8). With western help, Jugoslavia then withstood several years of pressure from the Soviet bloc. It cultivated links with third-world countries (7), and in 1961 the 'non-aligned' movement was founded at a conference in Belgrade.

Albania's links with the USSR (which had built submarine bases on its Mediterranean coast) were broken in 1961, but this did not bring it back into friendly relations with Jugoslavia. Albania's rulers accused the USSR of betraying the doctrines of Stalinism almost as shamefully as Jugoslavia had done; they sided with China, then under rigid Maoist rule, in its quarrel with the 'revisionist' Soviet rulers. But by 1978 China was abandoning Maoism: Albania broke with China, and throughout the 1980s this mountainous little country of 3 million people, isolated politically as well as physically, claimed to be the only true communist state. The condition of its people became even worse than that of the other communist Balkan states.

Meanwhile Jugoslavia was troubled by the problem of its own 2.25 million Albanians. Multinational Jugoslavia had been structured as a federation of six republics. The biggest, Serbia, included two 'autonomous

regions': in the north, Voivodina, whose population is partly Hungarian; in the south, Kosovo, with 2 million people, of whom over 80% are Albanian. (Albanians also make up a quarter of Macedonia's population of 2 million.) Violence broke out in Kosovo in 1968, and again, on a larger scale, in the early 1980s. Thousands of Serbs left the region, complaining of intimidation. Some Kosovo rioters had called for union with Albania, but the demand more often voiced was for Kosovo to be upgraded to the status of a republic within Jugoslavia. In 1989 Serbia's hard-line communist leaders imposed constitutional changes that stripped Kosovo and Voivodina of their autonomy, bringing them under direct Serbian rule from Belgrade. The Kosovo Albanians responded with waves of strikes and civil disobedience.

At the same time, rifts widened between Serbia and other republics. Jugoslavia's federal system had run smoothly when all-powerful communist bosses kept each republic in line. But the east European wind of change began to blow hard in Croatia, and harder in Slovenia. In early 1990 those two republics, the most 'western' culturally as well as geographically, ousted their former communist bosses when they held their first free elections; in December the Slovenes voted overwhelmingly, in a referendum, for secession from Jugoslavia. In Serbia, however, the hard-liners yielded on only one point: they renamed their communist party as socialist.

They held and won elections of dubious fairness, and started to use the Serbian predominance in the Jugoslav armed forces, and the presence of large Serbian minorities in Bosnia and Croatia, to curb the westerners' impatience for reform. The Serbs form 35% of Jugoslavia's total population of 24 million, provide 75% of its army officers, make up 30% of Bosnia's very mixed population (in which 44% are Muslim and 17% Croat) and have close traditional links with the Montenegrins. But, with all this strength, the Serbian leaders seemed to be alienating rather than cowing the Bosnians, Macedonians and other hesitant groups, and it was thought that Jugoslavia was more likely to fall apart than be held together under tough Serbian domination.

In 1990 even Albania began to feel the wind of change. Thousands of Albanians poured into foreign embassies in Tirana, and eventually the regime had to let them leave the country. After a series of student demonstrations the regime announced that 'independent' political parties would be authorized – but they were not to be permitted to campaign against the ruling communist party. At the same time Albania sought to restore relations with the USSR, China and the US. Its relations with Jugoslavia remained tense. With its other neighbour, Greece, it apparently could not decide how to find an accommodation. Many of the 350,000 Greeks in southern Albania would have escaped long ago if the frontier had not been closely guarded. In the last weeks of 1990 several thousands crossed into Greece safely, but hundreds of others were shot, electrocuted or bayoneted to death by the guards, whose behaviour changed from day to day.

18 Germany

In 1990, after more than 40 years of enforced separation, East Germany, formerly a Soviet 'satellite' state, was united with, and for most practical purposes merged into, a West Germany that was already the strongest economic power in Europe. Even so, the new united Germany was smaller than the country had been in 1937. The Nazi regime that held power in Germany from 1933 to 1945 had led it into a series of annexations and wars of conquest which, in the end, left it both smaller and divided.

In 1938 Nazi Germany occupied Austria – a German-speaking country, but one with a distinctive history and a strong cultural identity of its own. Then, after a four-power conference at Munich, Germany forced the cession of the German-peopled Sudetenland border region of western

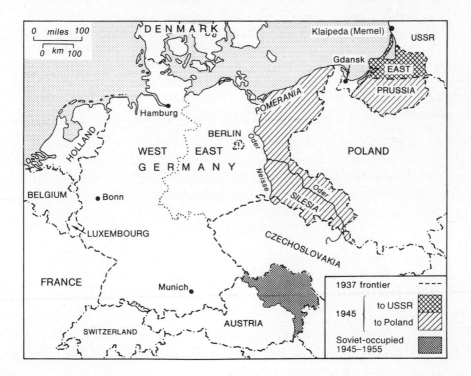

Czechoslovakia (running all along its frontier with Germany). In 1939 it took over the rest of Czechoslovakia; demanded Danzig (now Gdansk), which was then a 'free city', serving Poland as a port; and, using Danzig as a pretext, invaded Poland – after making a pact with the USSR under which the two powers then divided Poland between them. Britain and France, which had given guarantees to Poland, declared war on Germany. During the subsequent six years of war, Germany, with its allies, at one stage controlled most of Europe, including a large part of Russia. But by 1945 the Nazi empire was destroyed, and the advancing allied western and Soviet armies met in the middle of Germany.

Austria was re-established as a democratic republic, although the four main allied powers (Britain, France, USA, USSR) kept troops there until 1955. The Sudetenland was returned to Czechoslovakia and its German inhabitants were expelled. France took over the Saar – but returned it to Germany in 1957. The USSR annexed northern East Prussia and, expelling the inhabitants of Silesia and the other parts of Germany east of the line of the rivers Oder and Neisse, assigned these areas to Poland (*14*).

The Germany that remained was divided into four zones, each under the military administration of one of the four occupying powers. The old capital, Berlin, was also divided into sectors garrisoned by the four powers. The USSR imposed a communist regime on its zone and blocked western attempts to rebuild a democratic system for the whole of Germany. By 1948 the western allies had to give up hope of Soviet co-operation and put through reforms in their three zones alone. The USSR then blockaded West Berlin for a year, but a huge airlift mounted by the western allies kept its 2 million people fed (and even coal was flown in). In later years, particularly in the 1960s, the USSR often interfered with the west's communications with Berlin when it wanted to test the western governments' nerve, and to remind them of its military strength in central Europe.

The three western zones were united in 1949 to form the Federal Republic of Germany (FRG), with its capital at Bonn. The communist state created in the Soviet zone was called the German Democratic Republic (GDR). In the 1950s several million people escaped from East Germany (the GDR) to the west, many of them by way of Berlin. To stop this outflow, the GDR built a massive 30-mile-long wall between the two parts of Berlin in 1961, and created a 'death strip', with minefields, along the whole border between West and East Germany.

A large Soviet army, about 400,000 strong, remained in the GDR, which became a member of the Soviet-run Warsaw Pact (*13*). West Germany joined NATO in 1955 (*20*), and the allied forces there relinquished their

occupation status, but that status remained the basis of the presence of the British, French and US garrisons in West Berlin.

In the 1970s West Germany made treaties with the USSR, Poland and East Germany; and Britain, France, the USA and the USSR signed a new agreement on Berlin. But, although the Soviet and GDR governments signed the 1975 Helsinki agreement (*13*), they flouted it by denying the 17 million East Germans the right to free contact with the 62 million West Germans. In the late 1980s, when changes began in Poland, Hungary and the USSR itself, the East German communist regime rejected any idea of reform. In the end, however, it was swept away by the European tide.

West Germany began to receive floods of ethnic Germans who were at last able to leave eastern Europe and the USSR: 43,000 in 1986, 80,000 in 1987, 150,000 in 1988, 350,000 in 1989. Hundreds of frustrated East Germans, demanding permission to go west, camped in West German embassies in east European capitals. In September 1989 Hungary threw open its frontier with Austria, and thousands of East Germans poured across it. By November more than 200,000 East Germans had got out, through Hungary and otherwise. The GDR communists, in desperation, ditched their old leaders and opened the Berlin wall. But the outflow did not slacken until they promised a free election. This, held in March 1990, predictably put a non-communist government in power. It hastened to start talks about unification.

In October 1990 the GDR vanished into a united Germany. It was re-divided into the five *Länder* (states) that the communists had abolished; in the Federal Republic these took their places alongside the ten western states and Berlin. The whole of the new Germany was now within the European Community (*19*). The whole of it was also within NATO (*20*); the USSR had agreed to this, after a few months of negotiation, during which it emerged that the new east European governments saw a Germany in NATO as a more reassuring prospect than an uninhibited Germany left to its own devices. The Soviet forces in Germany were to be withdrawn by 1994; NATO would hold no manoeuvres in eastern Germany until they had gone; Germany would pay $6,000 million towards the cost of removing them. Germany confirmed its acceptance of the Oder–Neisse frontier and its renunciation of nuclear, chemical and biological weapons. These terms, contained in a treaty signed in Moscow in September, required ratification by Britain, France, the USA and the USSR as well as by Germany. There were various unresolved problems, and it was uncertain whether the gains and strains of unification would strengthen or weaken Germany in the next few years (*2, 19*), but a notable change in the map of Europe had been made, definitively and with spectacular speed.

19 West European unities

In 1947 most of the non-communist European countries joined the Organization for European Economic Co-operation (OEEC), which was formed to handle the European Recovery Programme (ERP, or Marshall Plan) that massive American aid made possible. The OEEC was succeeded in 1961 by the OECD (Organization for Economic Co-operation and Development), whose 24 members included, outside Europe, Australia, Canada, Japan, New Zealand and the United States. OECD headquarters are in Paris.

From 1949 on, most of the European democracies sent ministers and members of parliament to the Council of Europe at Strasbourg (*18*), a mainly consultative body. The conventions that it negotiated included one on human rights; to adjudicate on this, the European Court of Human Rights, also at Strasbourg, was established in 1959.

Western European Union (WEU) originated with the signing of the Brussels Treaty in 1948 by Britain, France, Belgium, Holland (the Netherlands) and Luxembourg. (The last three of these five had previously formed a customs union, known as Benelux.) Italy and West Germany joined WEU in 1955; Spain and Portugal joined in 1988. The 1948 treaty had reflected a disarmed post-war western Europe's fear of the large Soviet army in Germany, and of Soviet intentions as indicated by the 1948 coup in Czechoslovakia (*13*); WEU also provided a reassuring framework around the rearming of West Germany as a counter to the Soviet arming of East Germany (*18*). Most of WEU's functions were later absorbed into the work of NATO (*20*), but it was kept alive because some Europeans wanted a defence grouping independent of the US, either as a shield against American pressure or as something to cling to if the Americans should abandon Europe.

The European Economic Community (EEC), often called the Common Market, was based on the 1957 Treaty of Rome, signed by France, West Germany, Italy and the Benelux three. Trade between these Six was made duty-free by stages; the last tariffs were abolished in 1968. The Six had also created a European Coal and Steel Community (ECSC) and a European Atomic Energy Community (Euratom). They agreed to merge the three groupings into a single European Community (EC), and in 1967 the three executive bodies were replaced by a single European Commission, based in Brussels.

The Six adopted a common agricultural policy (CAP), freed the movement of labour between their countries and promoted integration in other ways. They established a European Parliament (at Strasbourg), whose powers were gradually increased, although the Council of Ministers retained ultimate authority in many matters.

Britain and other countries which did not want to go so far or so fast as the Six formed the European Free Trade Association (EFTA) in 1960, siting its headquarters in Geneva. By 1967 they had abolished all tariffs on (non-farm) trade among them. In 1973 Britain and Denmark left EFTA and joined the EC, and Ireland also joined it. Greece joined the EC in 1981, Spain and Portugal in 1986, making it a Community of 12 members. The remaining EFTA countries – Austria, Finland (formally an associate member), Iceland, Norway, Sweden and Switzerland – signed free-trade agreements with the EC in 1972–3. As a result, tariff-free trade in industrial goods was achieved between all 18 members of the two groups by 1984.

A 1963 convention signed at Yaoundé, in Cameroun, provided for development aid and access to EC markets for 18 associated African states. These arrangements were enlarged, and extended to 48 other African, Caribbean and Pacific (ACP) states, by subsequent conventions signed at Lomé, in Togo.

By 1990 Austria, Cyprus, Malta and Turkey had applied to join the Community. Sweden had declared its intention of joining; Norway seemed to like the idea of a joint application by Finland, Norway and Sweden. But the 12 EC members were holding back on new admissions. They needed to work out the consequences for them of the unifying of Germany; before it, West Germany was already the EC's strongest economy, and a united Germany would loom even larger (2, 18). They faced appeals for help from eastern Europe (13); they had agreed to provide $1,600 million worth of aid for the USSR In 1991. They had embarked, perhaps ambitiously, on intricate negotiations with the intention (at least in some minds) of achieving, within three years, three main aims: a 'single market' in which non-tariff restraints on trade (national subsidies, price-rigging, etc.) would be reduced, if not abolished; constitutional reforms, extending the EC's political role and possibly its parliament's powers; and the first stage of a plan for 'economic and monetary union' (EMU) which would lead, in three stages, to a single European currency – guarded by a single central bank.

Even among enthusiasts for European unity, some doubted whether the

Community could carry much new weight. Its existing operations had had some unhappy results – notably the CAP, with its costly subsidizing and tight protection of inefficient farming: the consequent creation of huge surpluses, which were 'dumped' in other markets, was gravely harmful to many of the world's efficient farmers. In 1990 the EC's refusal to make any big cuts in these subsidies was one main cause of the perilous deadlock reached in the world trade talks between members of the General Agreement on Tariffs and Trade (GATT).

20 Atlantic alliance

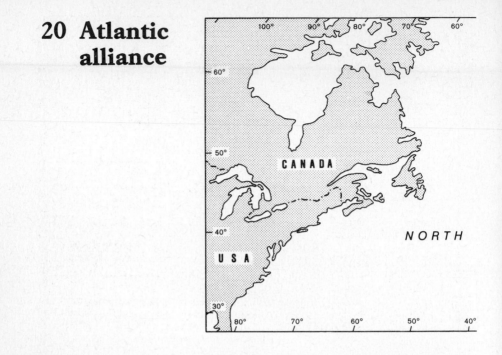

In 1948 the Brussels Treaty signatories (*19*) – Britain, France, Belgium, Holland and Luxembourg – being unable to counterbalance the military power that the USSR was maintaining in central Europe, sought American support. Traditional American dislike of 'entangling alliances' was overcome after several menacing Soviet moves – the coup in Czechoslovakia, the Berlin blockade, threats to Norway and Finland (*13, 21*). In 1949 the United States and Canada, the Brussels Treaty five, and Denmark, Iceland, Italy, Norway and Portugal signed the North Atlantic Treaty. The 12 allies pledged joint resistance to any attack, in Europe, on any of them. The invasion of South Korea (*58*) in 1950 increased the allies' fears, leading them to create a more elaborate North Atlantic Treaty Organization (NATO).

Greece and Turkey joined the alliance in 1952, West Germany in 1955; Spain became the sixteenth member in 1982. France withdrew its forces from NATO command in 1966 – without withdrawing from the treaty – and the headquarters of NATO and of its European command were moved from France to Belgium. In the 1970s disputes between Greece and Turkey affected their participation in NATO activities. Many other disputes arose, but the allies were periodically reminded of the need for their

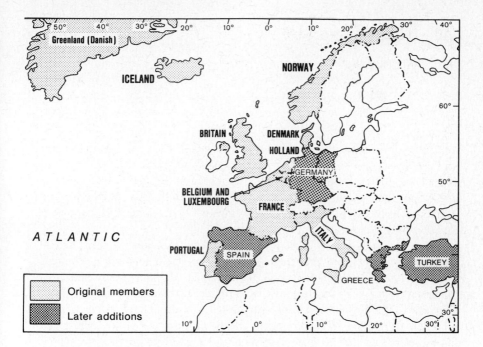

Original members

Later additions

alliance by disturbing Soviet actions (from the 1956 invasion of Hungary to the 1979–89 occupation of Afghanistan, *16, 49*).

In 1990 the USSR, which had previously insisted on a reunited Germany becoming 'neutral', agreed to the unifying of West and East Germany without that condition. The former East Germany thus became NATO territory, in which, however, Soviet troops were to remain until 1994.

With all the dramatic new changes in Europe (*13*), some people questioned the future of the alliance; in particular, it was expected that American public opinion would turn against keeping US troops in Europe. But it was also argued that Germany's new strength made it important for that strength to be kept within an international framework, which NATO might provide. Meanwhile the Atlantic alliance had already surpassed every other alliance in history, in its scale and its 41-year duration.

21 Scandinavia

Traditional Scandinavian neutrality was shattered by the Soviet invasion of Finland in 1939 and Nazi Germany's occupation of Denmark and Norway in 1940. The Finns, hoping to regain the territory the USSR had seized (*14*), joined the Germans in attacking it in 1941. Only Sweden remained neutral throughout the 1939–45 war. Britain prevented the Germans from extending their occupation of Denmark to Iceland, which became fully independent in 1944 (*11, 22*).

After 1945 a Nordic Council was created as a means of consultation between ministers and members of parliament from Denmark, Finland, Iceland, Norway and Sweden. A Scandinavian defence union was also proposed, but Denmark, Iceland and Norway, fearing that this would not give them enough security, joined the North Atlantic alliance in 1949 (*20*).

Their fears arose largely from the USSR's annexation of the three small Baltic states (*14*) and its grip on Poland and East Germany (*16, 18*), which brought the whole eastern shore of the Baltic under Soviet control. In the far north the USSR annexed Finland's Arctic port, Petsamo (now Pechenga), and built up large armed forces in the Kola peninsula (*22*). Porkkala, the base near Helsinki which it had occupied in 1944, was handed back to the Finns in 1956; but they had been forced to cede an eighth of all their territory to the USSR, and under a 1948 treaty they were committed to help defend the USSR if it were attacked across Finnish territory. In the 1980s Sweden was troubled by furtive intrusions into its coastal waters by submarines (one Soviet submarine ran aground near a Swedish naval base). In 1988, however, after 19 years of deadlock, caused by the USSR's refusal to take the Swedish island of Gotland into account, the two countries at last agreed on a Baltic dividing line (*6, 22*).

Soviet pressure on Finland blocked attempts in 1968–70 to form a Nordic economic union ('Nordek'). But Finland was able to become an associate member of EFTA (*19*) and, like other EFTA countries, to conclude a free-trade agreement with the EC in 1972. In 1973 Denmark joined the EC but retained its place in the Nordic Council and in other arrangements for Scandinavian co-operation. The self-governing Faroe islands (*22*) stayed out of the EC when Denmark joined; Greenland, after obtaining self-government, withdrew from the EC in 1985 (*11, 19*).

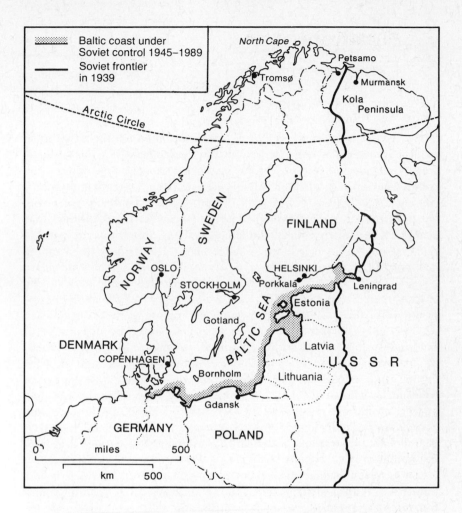

The dramatic changes in the Soviet sphere in 1989–90 transformed the situation in the Baltic region. The Nordic countries took a particular interest in the new developments in the USSR's Baltic republics. Of their many old links with those areas, the closest were Finland's with Estonia (the two languages have much in common).

22 Northern seas

The coastal states around the North Sea have shared out the rights to its sea bed oil and gas by drawing dividing lines based mainly on equidistance from coasts, on the authority of the 1958 international convention on the 'continental shelf' (6). Britain – largely thanks to its Shetland and Orkney islands – and Norway got most of the oil. Initially Germany got a very small sector, but in 1969 it obtained a ruling from the International Court at The Hague which obliged the Danes and the Dutch to cede parts of their sectors. Later, Britain and France adopted a dividing line running down the Channel, with the British Channel Islands in a small sea enclave on the French side of the line. Disputes continued about some of the British–Irish dividing lines. The Irish argued that baselines should not be drawn from small islands, and particularly not from the Rockall islet, which is uninhabitable but has been formally annexed by Britain. (Denmark, meanwhile, put in a claim that Rockall was an extension of the Faroes.)

The continental shelf is wide in this region; it underlies large sea areas around Britain and Ireland, as well as the whole of the North sea except for a narrow band of deeper water along Norway's coast. But the 1958 shelf convention did not resolve disputes over fishing rights. In the 1950s and 1960s Norway and Iceland, whose coastal fisheries had been much used by British and other trawlers, widened their fishing limits, setting off a series of disputes.

These quarrels affected Iceland's attitude to NATO, which it had joined as a founder member (20). Having no armed forces (and a population of only 240,000), its main contribution to the alliance was the providing of land for an air base at Keflavik, near Reykjavik; the special value of this base to the allies was that American aircraft flying from it could watch Soviet warships' movements into the Atlantic from Murmansk (11, 21). During the 1950s Iceland began to make deals with the USSR, exchanging fish for Soviet oil, and asked the Americans to withdraw from Keflavik. After long negotiations, however, the NATO base was retained. In the 1970s Iceland extended its fishing limits first to 50 miles from shore and then to 200 miles, and had a series of (bloodless) 'cod wars' with Britain, whose fishing fleet was particularly hard hit by exclusion from Icelandic and Norwegian waters.

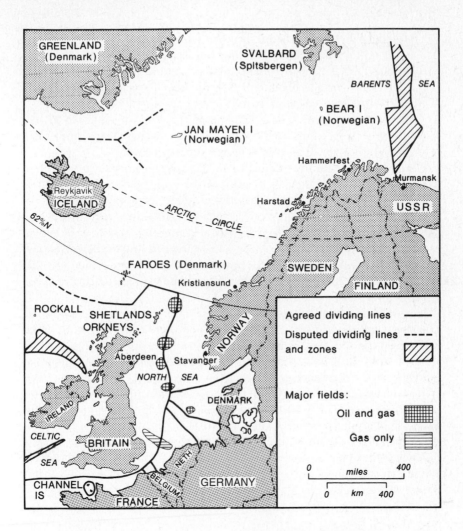

Many states announced claims to mineral and fishing rights in 200-mile 'exclusive economic zones' (EEZs) along their coasts during the 1970s (6). The member states of the EC (19) proclaimed a joint EEZ. In the North Sea this joint zone roughly corresponded to all the 'oil sectors' combined, except Norway's. Britain, which 'contributed' the largest part of the zone and of the stocks of fish in it, would not accept the idea that all EC member states should have unrestricted fishing rights throughout the joint EEZ. Wrangling among EC members over fishing quotas was virtually continuous until an agreement was concluded in 1983.

Farther north, when Norway proclaimed a 200-mile zone for its Jan Mayen island, disputes about dividing lines arose with Denmark (because of Greenland, *21*) and with Iceland. Norway had a more serious dispute with the USSR over the dividing line in the Barents Sea, which is rich in fish and may prove rich in oil. Norway proposed a median line, based on equidistance from coasts. The USSR argued that lines of longitude should be used as basis for what, in their view, was an Arctic 'sector' boundary. The difference involved an area of 60,000 square miles.

The same two countries were also at odds over Svalbard (Spitsbergen). Under a 1920 treaty this island group was acknowledged to be Norwegian territory, but other nations were given the right to exploit its resources on the basis of equal access under Norwegian law. Both Norway and the USSR have mined coal there. The Soviet contention was that all signatories of the 1920 treaty ought to have similar access to the sea bed resources of Svalbard's continental shelf (which may include exploitable oil). Norway claimed that the Svalbard shelf should be treated as part of its own shelf.

Norway had kept a wary eye on the Soviet mining camps in Svalbard for fear that a military presence might be created there. (In the late 1940s the USSR had tried to make Norway let it station a garrison in Svalbard.) For its part, the USSR had strategic motives for discouraging other nations' activities in the Barents Sea. It wanted to keep foreigners well away from its naval bases around Murmansk in the Kola peninsula. Its warships and submarines could enter the Atlantic without having to pass through the Baltic or Mediterranean straits by using these bases, which are ice-free (*10*, *11*) – the effect of the Gulf Stream and its continuation in the North Atlantic Drift being to extend ice-free water far north of the Arctic Circle in these northern seas.

23 Minorities and micro-states

In western Europe some linguistic disputes and separatist demands have led to violent clashes, others to mainly political action (while extremist groups have used violence on the fringes of many non-violent movements). For similar problems in eastern Europe see *14–17*.

Belgium is almost equally divided between two language groups. Flemish, a variant of Dutch, is spoken mainly north of a line running just south of the (bilingual) capital, Brussels. French is spoken mainly in the south, which is sometimes called Wallonia. Historically, French was long dominant; but the Walloons are outnumbered, and economic power has shifted to the Flemish north. Constitutional changes in the 1970s introduced wide regional autonomy, but this did not end the friction. Some Flemings and some Walloons still voice separatist aims.

In *Britain*, Scottish and Welsh nationalists made headway in elections in the 1960s and 1970s. In 1979 referendums were held on proposals for devolution, with a separate assembly for each country. The voting was negative in Wales and indecisive in Scotland. The proposals lapsed, but some nationalist agitation continued, the Welsh movement focusing on language rights, while some Scots had North Sea oil (*22*) particularly in mind. The Channel Islands and the Isle of Man have long enjoyed autonomy. For *Ireland* see *24*.

In *France* elected councils were created in all the 22 regions during the 1980s, after years of sometimes violent agitation in Corsica and Brittany; in the Languedoc area there had also been much discontent with the centralized French administrative system. The Basques in France had been affected by the struggles involving their neighbours in Spain, and in the mid-1980s a smaller separatist movement of French Basques began a campaign of violence.

In *Spain* old regional rights were suppressed during General Franco's dictatorship (see also *25*), and a violent nationalist movement developed in the Basque provinces. After Franco's death a plan for regional autonomy was adopted, starting with the Basque provinces and Catalonia, which elected assemblies in 1980; but some Basque groups aiming at complete independence continued to use violence, although nearly all other Basques now condemned this persistence in terrorism.

Switzerland is a federation whose 23 cantons have wide autonomy, and this has helped to reduce fiction between the German-speaking majority and the minorities who speak French and Italian. (About 50,000 Swiss still speak an old local language, Romansh.) In 1978, however, a new Jura canton had to be created to end a long period of agitation in a French-speaking area which had been included, since 1815, in the German-speaking Berne canton.

Italy now has a system of regional autonomy. It has faced a special problem in the area which, before 1918, was part of Austria and known as South Tirol but was then transferred to Italy and called Alto Adige, or the provinces of Bolzano (Bozen) and Trento (Trent). Two-thirds of Bolzano's inhabitants speak German, and their resentment at being lumped together with Trento led to some terrorist violence and friction between Italy and Austria. In 1972 Bolzano was given separate autonomy.

Luxembourg, a grand duchy with 370,000 people, uses three languages: French, German and its own dialect, Letzeburgesch. The map shows several even smaller states, with populations in the 20,000 to 35,000 range: Andorra, Liechtenstein, Monaco and San Marino (there is also the tiny Vatican City state in Rome). They have economic and other links with larger neighbours – Luxembourg with Belgium, Andorra with France and Spain, Liechtenstein with Switzerland, Monaco with France, San Marino and the Vatican state with Italy – but they are sovereign states. Luxembourg was a founder member of the United Nations; Liechtenstein joined the UN in 1990. These two, with Monaco, San Marino and the Vatican state, took part in the 'Helsinki process' series of CSCE meetings (*13*) from the beginning.

Since 1945 minority problems of a new kind have arisen as a result of large-scale immigration into western Europe from other continents. Too widely dispersed to be clearly shown on a map of this kind, these new immigrants are, however, mainly concentrated in big cities, and some prominent groups among them may be briefly noted: in Britain, those from southern Asia (India, Pakistan and Bangladesh) and the West Indies; in France – and, more recently, in Italy too – those from the Arab countries of North Africa (*38*); in Germany, those from the Asian part of Turkey; in Holland, Ambonese from Indonesia (*63*) and other refugees from Surinam (*71*). One result of the new migration has been the growth of large Muslim communities (*28*) in Europe, especially in Britain and France.

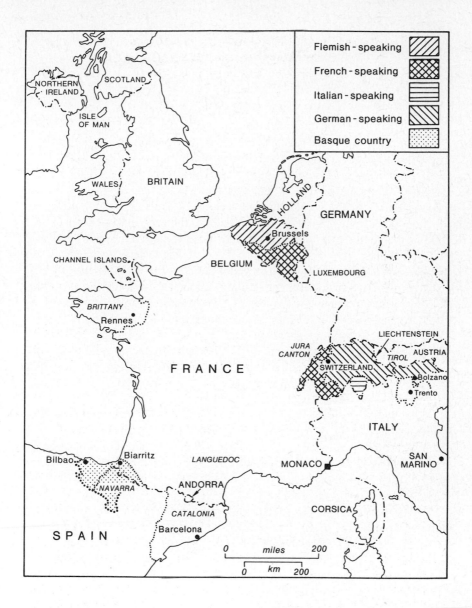

Flemish - speaking
French - speaking
Italian - speaking
German - speaking
Basque country

NORTHERN IRELAND
SCOTLAND
ISLE OF MAN
WALES
BRITAIN
CHANNEL ISLANDS
BRITTANY
Rennes

HOLLAND
GERMANY
BELGIUM
Brussels
LUXEMBOURG

LIECHTENSTEIN
JURA CANTON
TIROL
AUSTRIA
SWITZERLAND
Bolzano
Trento

FRANCE

ITALY

Bilbao
Biarritz
LANGUEDOC
MONACO
SAN MARINO
NAVARRA
ANDORRA
CATALONIA
CORSICA
SPAIN
Barcelona

0   miles   200
0   km   200

24 Ireland

The state that is usually called Britain, for short, in this book is formally the United Kingdom of Great Britain and Northern Ireland. It was the UK of Great Britain and Ireland from 1801 until, after a bloody guerrilla war in Ireland, it was partitioned by the 1921 treaty. That treaty gave effective independence to the greater part of Ireland – which was later, in 1949, declared a republic – but it left six counties of the province of Ulster in the UK, with a 'home rule' system and a Northern Ireland parliament at Stormont in Belfast.

The republic's constitution asserted a claim to the whole island. But in Northern Ireland (population 1.6 million, about 37% Catholic) the Protestant majority showed by their voting in every election that they had no wish to be taken over by the republic, whose population of 3.5 million is almost wholly Catholic, and whose main traditions are of resistance to British rule. Meanwhile Irish migration to Britain continued; movement across the border was unrestricted; at times the 'Irish Republican Army' (IRA) and other terrorist groups made raids into 'the north' from bases in 'the south'.

In the 1960s the prime ministers in Dublin and Belfast joined in trying to improve relations, with support from Britain, which made a free-trade pact with the republic. But a backlash in 1969 led to communal clashes in Belfast, Londonderry and other towns. British troops were sent to restore order when Northern Ireland's own police failed to protect Catholics against Protestant mobs' attacks.

Attempts to arrange 'power-sharing' between the north's Protestant and Catholic politicians failed; 'home rule', which had always produced Stormont governments based on Protestant parties, was abandoned; the province was ruled directly from London after 1974, which eased the Catholic minority's position. In the 1985 'Hillsborough agreement' Britain promised to give the Dublin government some say in Northern Irish affairs, although this set off new waves of Protestant anger. Deaths in Northern Ireland resulting from terrorism, which numbered nearly 2,000 in the 1970s, declined to fewer than 800 in the 1980s (in 1990 there were 76). But the extension of IRA terrorism to Britain, including the 1984 'Brighton bomb' attempt to kill the Prime Minister, increased unease among the

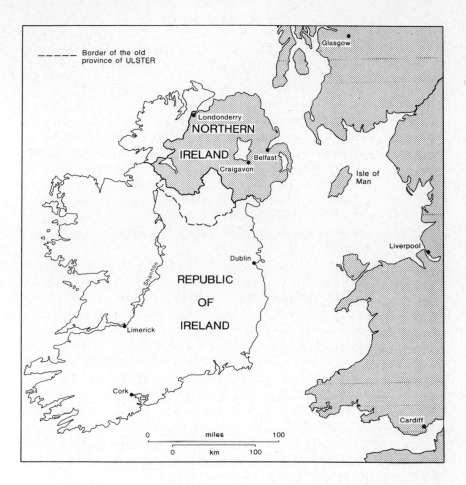

Border of the old province of ULSTER

Glasgow

Londonderry

NORTHERN

IRELAND

Belfast

Craigavon

Isle of Man

Liverpool

Dublin

Shannon

REPUBLIC

OF

IRELAND

Limerick

Cork

Cardiff

0   miles   100

0   km   100

millions of Irish living there. In 1988 the IRA, strengthened by gifts from Libya (*38*) of arms, explosives and money, began an 'international' campaign of murders in several European countries; although claiming to aim only at British soldiers, it killed civilians of various nationalities.

25 Gibraltar

For 250 years Gibraltar was one of Britain's most valuable naval bases. When the Suez route became an imperial lifeline, Gibraltar and Malta were important staging posts along it (*41*). Malta became independent in 1964. For Gibraltar, however, independence did not seem a practical goal. Although its population was as large as that of such micro-states as Andorra or San Marino (*23*), it was only a narrow four-mile-long peninsula, dominated by the spectacular Rock, and also overshadowed by Spain's recurring demands for it.

Captured by Britain in 1704 (and later renounced by Spain in exchange for Florida), Gibraltar was thus held by Britain longer than it had been held by Spain, which had not taken it from the Moors until 1462. When the Gibraltarians were given fuller internal self-government in 1964, Spain began to try to force them to accept its rule. The Spanish government – then controlled by the dictator, General Francisco Franco – barred trade with Gibraltar, threatened to impede its air and sea communications, and obstructed frontier crossings, stopping them completely from 1969 onward. The Gibraltarians were not cowed. In a 1967 referendum they voted almost unanimously to retain their links with Britain, and they confirmed this decision by their votes in each subsequent election for their House of Assembly (in those days the only freely elected legislature in the Iberian peninsula). Gibraltar's economy suffered from the 'siege', but the adjacent region in Spain was much harder hit.

General Franco died in 1975, but the 'siege' continued, mainly because of the Spanish army's pressure on the new elected governments in Spain, which at first were visibly fragile. In 1982 Spain began to permit frontier crossings under restrictive conditions, but the frontier was not fully re-opened until 1985, shortly before Spain joined the EC (*19*).

Although Spain had argued that it was intolerable for a country to have a foreign enclave on its coast, it continued to hold two enclaves on the coast of Morocco – Ceuta and Melilla, the last places in Africa still ruled by a European state (*39*). Morocco indicated that it would raise the question of these two '*presidios*' if Gibraltar were to be transferred to Spanish control.

26 Cyprus, Greece and Turkey

Cyprus was ruled by Turkey from 1570 to 1878, then by Britain until 1960, but four-fifths of its 500,000 people were Greek. In 1960 it became independent, with a constitution designed to give the Turkish minority a share of power. Britain retained two sovereign base areas; Greece and Turkey kept small forces in Cyprus; all three countries had the right, by treaty, to intervene to maintain Cyprus's constitutional arrangements. The constitution broke down, fighting spread, and the Turkish Cypriots were driven into small enclaves. In 1964 war between Greece and Turkey seemed imminent, and a United Nations force manned by seven nations (including Britain) was installed in Cyprus. For ten years the UN men prevented clashes from escalating, but talks about a settlement became deadlocked and the Turks stayed in their enclaves, which included the northern half of the capital, Nicosia.

In 1974 the military regime then ruling Greece organized a military coup in Cyprus, with the aim of annexing it to Greece. Turkish forces then occupied the north of the island. Greek and Turkish Cypriots fled or were driven across the new dividing line until hardly any Turks remained in the south or Greeks in the north. In Greece the military regime collapsed and democracy was restored. The Greek Cypriots' former government was also restored, and the Turkish Cypriots set up a government in the north.

The UN policed a new buffer zone between the two sides, but could not get them to agree on a settlement. The Greek Cypriot leaders wanted a united Cyprus, the Turkish ones a loose federation. Turkey's troops remained in the north, where the 'Turkish Republic of Northern Cyprus' was proclaimed in 1983.

In the Aegean Sea, Greece holds most of the islands that lie along Turkey's coast. Disputes over sea claims in the Aegean have caused several crises in Greek–Turkish relations. Turkey would have little freedom of movement in the Aegean, or access to its fisheries and oil potential, if Greece were to obtain 12-mile territorial waters and full continental shelf and EEZ rights for all its islands (6).

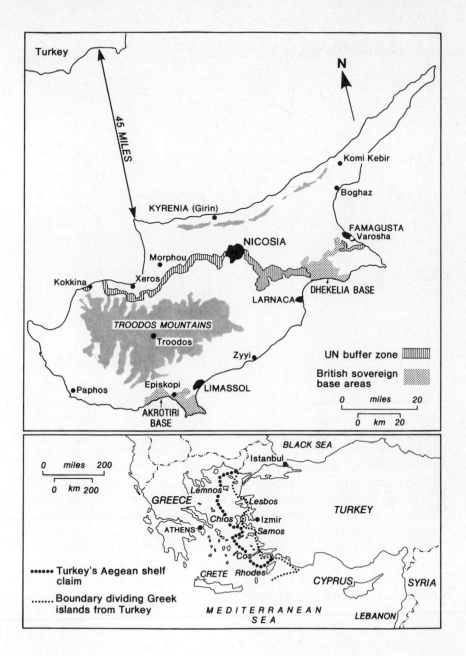

Turkey

N

45 MILES

Komi Kebir

Boghaz

KYRENIA (Girin)

FAMAGUSTA
Varosha

Morphou

NICOSIA

Kokkina

Xeros

DHEKELIA BASE

LARNACA

TROODOS MOUNTAINS

Troodos

Zyyi

UN buffer zone

British sovereign
base areas

Paphos

Episkopi

LIMASSOL

0   miles   20

AKROTIRI
BASE

0   km   20

BLACK SEA

Istanbul

0   miles   200

0   km   200

Lemnos

GREECE

Lesbos

TURKEY

Chios

Izmir

ATHENS

Samos

Cos

•••••• Turkey's Aegean shelf
claim

CRETE

Rhodes

CYPRUS

SYRIA

.... Boundary dividing Greek
islands from Turkey

MEDITERRANEAN
SEA

LEBANON

27 Asia and Africa

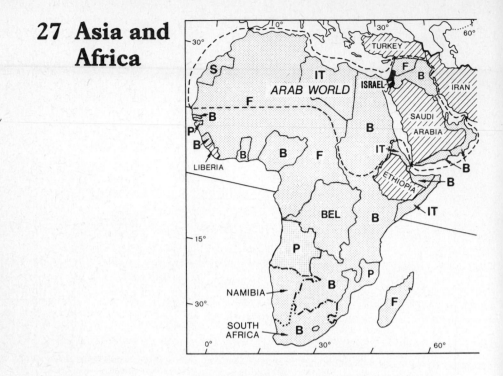

The map of these two continents has been transformed since 1945 by a rapid process of 'decolonization'. Before the 1939–45 war there were only a dozen sovereign states in the Afro-Asian world; now there are almost 100. Only a few small vestiges remain of the colonial empires that had been created by west European countries since the Portuguese first penetrated the Indian Ocean region in the 1490s. The building up of those empires had taken about 400 years, but they vanished in less than 40 years. Although their ending followed long and bloody struggles in some places, the most remarkable thing about this uniquely big and swift change in the world map was that the transfer of power was made by negotiation and without war in the majority of the former colonies and dependencies.

Most of the transformation was in fact carried out within a period of only 20 years, starting in 1946–7, when India, Pakistan and the Philippines became independent. But Portugal, the original pioneer among the west European empire-builders in Asia and Africa, was the slowest of them to relinquish its hold, and did not concede independence to its territories until after its own 1974 revolution, which ended a long period of authoritarian rule. Then, when it stopped trying to hold Angola and Mozambique,

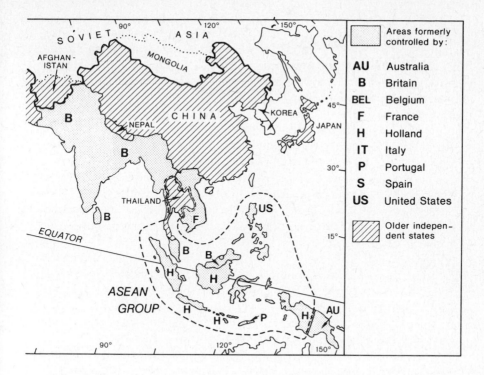

its withdrawal from southern Africa opened a door through which Zimbabwe and Namibia advanced to independence some years later (*31*, *34*).

Only one European power, the USSR, retained control of a large area in Asia. During the nineteenth century the tsarist Russian empire had pushed its frontiers southward by conquering independent Muslim states in central Asia and, farther east, taking territory from China. Its Soviet successors had to reconquer central Asia between 1918 and 1924, as the region's Muslim peoples had taken advantage of Russia's 1917 revolutions, and the subsequent chaos and civil war, to try to regain their freedom (*53*). Farther east, the Buryat Mongols were similarly reconquered, and the present Mongolian republic was effectively taken over by the USSR in 1924, although it was formally proclaimed an independent state. Elsewhere in Asia and Africa, the USSR fought a long but unsuccessful war in Afghanistan in 1979–89 and, using Cuban troops as proxies, established itself for a time as the patron of client regimes in Angola and Ethiopia; but its influence there, and in Indochina, was reduced when it could no longer keep up massive subsidies to the local rulers (*34, 35, 49, 60*).

A 'summit' conference of Asian and African governments (including China's but not Japan's) was held in 1955 at Bandung in Indonesia. But an attempt to repeat this at Algiers in 1965 was a fiasco: the host, Algeria's president, was deposed in an untimely coup, and as more and more 'new nations' joined the group many conflicting interests were emerging. Most of the Asian and African states joined the 'non-aligned' movement (7), but in practice they were more likely to get into disputes with the west than with the Soviet bloc: western colonialism was familiar to them, while the Soviet type was remote and disguised; as to economic aid and favourable trade rights, much more was expected from the west, because, here again, it was a familiar bargaining partner. There was particular resentment, among the African states, at each sign of western support for South Africa's white rulers; among the Arab states, at each sign of western support for Israel (33, 42–4).

However, the rift between China and the USSR complicated matters, especially when the two communist powers openly backed warring rivals in the Afro-Asian world – China siding with Pakistan and Cambodia, the USSR with India and Vietnam (51, 61). In south-east Asia the ASEAN group (59) was at times anxious for western support against possible pressure from either China or Vietnam. As Japan became an intensively industrialised economic superpower its attitudes ceased to have anything in common with those of 'third-world' Asian and African states, and this began to apply also to the east Asian 'little dragons' or 'newly industrial-ized countries' (54).

Most of the Afro-Asian world lined up against the USSR when it tried to enlarge its veto powers in the United Nations in the 1960s (by replacing the UN secretary-general with a three-man 'troika'). Most of it condemned the Soviet invasion of Afghanistan in 1979, and in 1990 most of it supported the UN resolutions that condemned Iraq's occupation of Kuwait and called for combined action to end it. The record did not support the idea that the new nations of Asia and Africa were obsessively hostile to the west on all issues and at all times.

28 Islam

The Muslims' religion originated in Arabia, and was first spread by Arab conquests, 1,300 years ago. Its scriptures are in Arabic, and its holiest shrine is at Mecca, in Saudi Arabia; thousands of Muslims make the pilgrimage (*haj*) there each year. But the vast majority of the world's 1,000 million Muslims are not Arabs. For instance, India, Pakistan and Bangladesh contain more Muslims than all the Arab countries put together. Moreover, not all Arabs are Muslims: there are large Christian communities in several Arab states.

Countries with Muslim majorities range from Senegal in West Africa to Indonesia in the Far East. Significant Muslim minorities include those in the USSR (over 50 million) and in China (about 40 million). Within a few years the rapidly growing Muslim population in central Asia and the Caucasus may amount to a quarter of the whole Soviet population.

In historical perspective, the power of Islam was at its height in the days when Muslim rulers controlled the Balkans, southern Russia, all of central Asia and most of India – before the expansion of European, Russian and Chinese power. But there has recently been a resurgence of Islam's importance in world affairs. Many of the new sovereign states that emerged from the old west European empires in Asia and Africa (*27*) were peopled and ruled by Muslims. The oil crises of the 1970s gave new international leverage to several Muslim states (*3, 40*). In some areas, Muslim fundamentalism – sometimes allied with leftist political forces, sometimes competing with them – has revived strongly, often in reaction against modernizing policies which have been denounced as alien 'westernizing' ones. A dramatic example was the 1979 revolution in Iran (*47*).

The Islamic Conference Organization (ICO), founded in 1969, had 46 member governments by the 1980s. Most of them could unite, at least in principle, in supporting the Palestinian Arabs against Israel and the Afghan resistance against the Soviet invasion of 1979 (*42, 49*). But some of them were alarmed at the way others tried to use Islamic appeals to extend their power: Libya, Iran and, by 1990, Iraq had all done this (*38, 45*).

Like other religions, Islam has sectarian divisions. The biggest one has long divided the Shias (about 120 million) from the orthodox Sunni majority. Iran has been a stronghold of Shia power for four centuries.

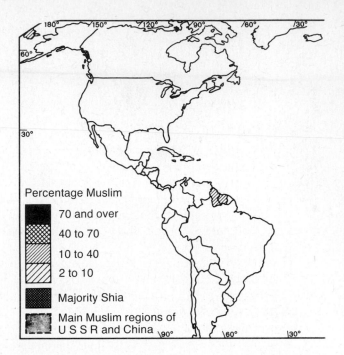

Percentage Muslim
- 70 and over
- 40 to 70
- 10 to 40
- 2 to 10
- Majority Shia
- Main Muslim regions of U S S R and China

Since 1979 it has had a strong influence on Shias in Lebanon (*44*), Kashmir (*51*) and some other areas; but it failed, during the 1980–8 Iran–Iraq war, to win over many of the Shias in Iraq, who outnumber the Sunnis there – although Iraq's present rulers are Sunnis (*48*).

Although Iran became conspicuous, after 1979, as a country ruled by fanatical fundamentalists, neither Iran nor the Shias have a monopoly of fanatical fundamentalism in the modern world of Islam. Several Arab governments have had cause to fear the Muslim Brotherhood, an organization founded in Egypt in 1928. Libya's rulers, since its 1969 coup, have favoured the employment of fanatical assassins (*38*). In Algeria and elsewhere, fundamentalist parties have gained support by exploiting discontent with the performance of long-established ruling groups. In 1989–90 there was particular indignation in Britain at the way an author living there was forced to go into hiding when an Iranian imam, branding a book of his (unread) as blasphemous, ordered Muslims to murder him and many Muslims in Britain approved of the order. This Salman Rushdie affair was a disturbing revelation of the width of the gulf of mutual incomprehension between Europeans and the large Muslim communities established in western Europe in recent years (*23*).

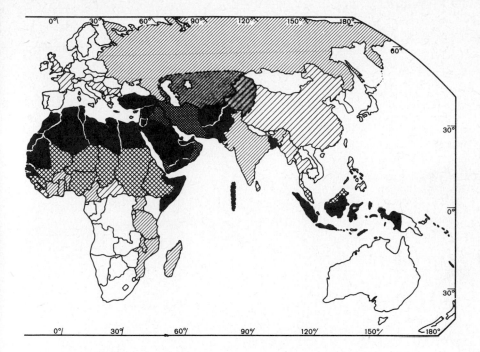

Throughout the Iran–Iraq war Iran had claimed to be fighting a Muslim holy war (*jihad*) against an infidel or heretical Iraqi regime. Iran's 700,000 war dead were 'martyrs' who had given their lives in a (vain) effort to liberate such Islamic holy places in Iraq as Karbala (*48*). But in 1990, when Iraq invaded and occupied Kuwait, a fellow Arab and fellow Muslim state, it also claimed to be engaged in a *jihad* and appealed for world-wide Muslim support – even though the troops lined up against it included soldiers from Arab Syria and Egypt, Muslim Pakistan and Bangladesh, and Saudi Arabia itself, the guardian of holy Mecca (*29*).

29 The Arab world

The Arabic language links about 215 million people inhabiting a belt that runs from the Atlantic to the Indian Ocean. Most Arabs are Muslims, and Mecca, Islam's holiest place, is in Saudi Arabia: so politicians and rulers seeking pan-Arab support often try to exploit Islamic sentiment (*28*). But Arab nationalism has mainly been a common reaction against alien rule – first by the old Turkish empire and then by west Europeans – and, since 1948, against the existence of a Jewish state, Israel, at a central position among the Arab states (*42*).

The Arab League was founded in 1945 by Egypt, Iraq, Jordan, Lebanon, Saudi Arabia, Syria and Yemen. By the 1980s they had been joined by Algeria, Bahrain, Djibouti, Kuwait, Libya, Mauritania, Morocco, Oman, Qatar, Somalia, Sudan, Tunisia and the United Arab Emirates (UAE); the Palestine Liberation Organization (PLO) had also been accepted as a member (*42*). The headquarters were sited in Cairo – Egypt being the most populous and central state – but were moved to Tunis when the League suspended Egypt from membership after its 1979 peace treaty with Israel (*43*). Egypt was readmitted in 1989, and it was agreed in principle that League headquarters should return to Cairo.

No clear line marks the Arab world's southern border. Although Djibouti, Somalia and Mauritania have joined the League, they were not usually included among the Arab states before they did so. The southern Sudan is neither Muslim nor Arab (*35*). In the Maghreb (west) the Berber language, which predates the eighth-century Arab conquest, survives in

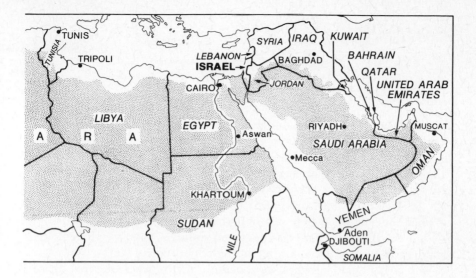

parts of Algeria and Morocco. In the east, northern Iraq is still peopled mainly by Kurds, despite the regime's efforts to eliminate them (*45*).

In 1990 Yemen and the former South Yemen (Aden) were united (*45*). Seven small Gulf states had formed the UAE in 1971–2 (*46*). Several other attempts to merge Arab states have failed. The merger of Egypt and Syria as the United Arab Republic (UAR) in 1958 lasted only until 1961. Libya's ruler, Colonel Qaddafi, has often announced its 'union' with some other Arab state, but none of these projects has taken shape.

Sub-regional groupings have developed. In 1981 Saudi Arabia and its small eastern neighbours formed the Gulf Co-operation Council (*46*). In 1989 the western group formed the Arab Maghreb Union (*38*). But the Arab Co-operation Council, also formed in 1989, was blown apart when one of its four members, Iraq, invaded Kuwait in 1990; Egypt, the other principal member, promptly sent troops to join the anti-Iraq line-up; Yemen went into diplomatic convulsions; Jordan, forced into an agonizing 'front-line' role, took the brunt of a flood of refugees from Iraq and Kuwait (*45*).

A shared nationalism has not saved the Arab states from continuous quarrelling. During the Iran–Iraq war (*48*) Syria and Libya even sided with Iran against Arab Iraq. But Iraq's swoop on Kuwait marked the first attempt by one Arab League state to seize another by force.

30 Africa

In Africa, European colonization and decolonization were both rapid (*27*). Until the 'scramble for Africa' in the 1880s, Europeans had controlled only a few coastal strips and some areas in the extreme north and south (*33, 38*). Then, within one century, nearly all of Africa came under European rule and re-emerged. Long guerrilla wars preceded the liberation of Algeria, Rhodesia and the Portuguese-held territories; most of the other states attained independence more peacefully, and in 1977 it came to Djibouti, the last part of 'black Africa' to be ruled from Europe (*35*). By 1990 the 'wind of change' was even blowing through South Africa (*33*).

Several hundred languages are spoken in Africa (where deserts, dense forests and lack of navigable rivers still impede communications), and many of the new states have been troubled by antagonisms between tribes. The Organization for African Unity, founded in 1963, has discouraged secessions (most OAU member states fear that, although the present frontiers are relics of the colonial period, to change them might lead to general fragmentation). In the 1980s some meetings of the OAU itself were disrupted by two particularly divisive issues: Morocco's occupation of Western Sahara (*39*) and Libya's attempts to dominate Chad and other states south of the Sahara (*37, 38*).

Recent conflicts have driven more than 5 million Africans across frontiers and into refugee camps. Droughts and civil wars combined in the 1980s to produce severe famine in some countries, notably Ethiopia, Mozambique and Sudan (*32, 35*); in West Africa the Sahara desert crept farther south into the 'Sahel' borderlands. As a whole, black Africa, which in the 1960s was keeping food production abreast of population growth and slowly raising its living standards, had become poorer by the mid-1980s, and acutely dependent on food aid from America and Europe. In the late 1980s several African governments recognised that the main cause of these ills was their own policies, which, while failing to discourage rising rates of population growth, had sharply discouraged production both of food and of exportable crops which could have earned foreign exchange. Signs began to appear that, in some countries, new policies – intended to give farmers more incentives – were having results. But food output per head was still 20% below the 1960s level.

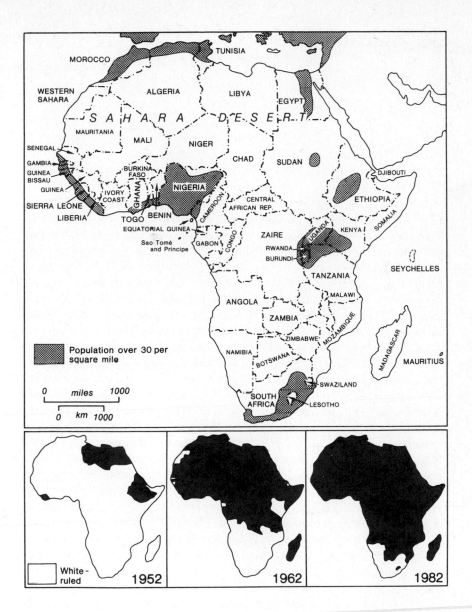

Population over 30 per square mile

0   miles   1000

0   km   1000

MOROCCO
TUNISIA
WESTERN SAHARA
ALGERIA
LIBYA
EGYPT
S A H A R A   D E S E R T
MAURITANIA
MALI
NIGER
CHAD
SUDAN
DJIBOUTI
SENEGAL
GAMBIA
GUINEA BISSAU
GUINEA
BURKINA FASO
GHANA
NIGERIA
ETHIOPIA
SIERRA LEONE
IVORY COAST
TOGO
BENIN
CAMEROON
CENTRAL AFRICAN REP.
SOMALIA
LIBERIA
EQUATORIAL GUINEA
Sao Tomé and Principe
GABON
CONGO
ZAIRE
UGANDA
KENYA
RWANDA
BURUNDI
SEYCHELLES
TANZANIA
MALAWI
ANGOLA
ZAMBIA
MOZAMBIQUE
ZIMBABWE
MADAGASCAR
MAURITIUS
NAMIBIA
BOTSWANA
SWAZILAND
SOUTH AFRICA
LESOTHO

White-ruled   1952

1962

1982

91

31 Southern Africa

The period of European rule had ended in most of Africa north of the equator by 1962, when France withdrew from Algeria (*30*, *38*), but it continued in the continent's southern part, which was strongly influenced by the Republic of South Africa (RSA), ruled by its large white minority (*33*). Portugal's government was determined to retain Angola and Mozambique, despite the guerrilla war that had begun in Angola. Southern Rhodesia (now Zimbabwe), nominally a British colony, was in practice ruled by its small white minority; the original white settlement there had been made from South Africa.

The mineral wealth of southern Africa (chrome, coal, cobalt, copper, diamonds, gold, manganese, nickel, platinum, titanium, uranium and other metals) was one cause of the creation of white communities there. Another was the existence of healthy highland areas where commercial crops could be grown (e.g. coffee in Angola and Kenya, tobacco in Rhodesia).

In the mid-1960s white dominance in the region began to yield. In 1963 Kenya became independent; a white-backed secession in Zaire's mineral-rich Katanga province (now Shaba) was ended by UN action; and Britain dissolved the Central African Federation that it had created in 1953 (*32*, *35*). Africans had come to regard the federation merely as a means for Southern Rhodesia's whites to extend their control over Northern Rhodesia and Nyasaland – which, as Zambia and Malawi, become independent in 1964.

In 1965 Southern Rhodesia's whites proclaimed an independent republic, which the RSA supported against international economic pressure and African guerrilla resistance; but its position grew weaker after Angola and Mozambique became independent in 1975, and in 1980 a new black government of Zimbabwe took over (*32*).

Pressure on the RSA to grant independence to Namibia (*34*) was increased in the 1980s, especially by the USA. South African troops withdrew, an election was held in 1989 under UN supervision, and in 1990 Namibia became independent.

The Southern African Development Co-ordination Conference (SADCC) was created in 1980 by Angola, Botswana, Mozambique, Tanzania, Zambia and Zimbabwe (the six 'front-line' states), together with Lesotho, Malawi and Swaziland. The main aim was to reduce the region's economic dependence on the RSA.

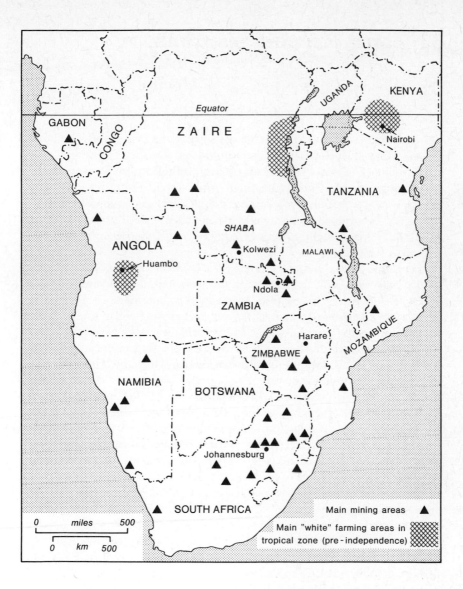

GABON

CONGO

GABON

ZAIRE

Equator

UGANDA

KENYA

Nairobi

TANZANIA

SHABA

Kolwezi

ANGOLA

Huambo

MALAWI

Ndola

ZAMBIA

MOZAMBIQUE

Harare

ZIMBABWE

NAMIBIA

BOTSWANA

Johannesburg

SOUTH AFRICA

| 0 | *miles* | 500 |

| 0 | *km* | 500 |

Main mining areas ▲

Main "white" farming areas in
tropical zone (pre-independence)

32 Zaire, Zambia, Zimbabwe

Zaire has only a narrow outlet to the sea; Zambia and Zimbabwe are land-locked. Mining development in these countries was made possible (*31*) by the building of railways from South Africa and from ports in Angola and Mozambique (both Portuguese-ruled until 1975). From 1960 onward, events were much influenced by the inland states' dependence on these routes. In the 1970s the Tanzania–Zambia (Tazara, or Tanzam) line was built, with Chinese help, to reduce Zambia's dependence on routes then still under white control.

Zaire, the former Belgian Congo, was granted independence in 1960 hastily and with little preparation. Its troops mutinied, and anarchy spread. Belgium sent troops in to protect the 110,000 whites; the UN sent an international force to restore order and ensure the Belgian troops' withdrawal. But in the mineral-rich Katanga province (now Shaba) a secessionist state was established, backed by local Belgian interests and with some support from Rhodesia and South Africa. The central government, in Leopoldville (now Kinshasa), disintegrated, and a rival Soviet-backed regime was installed at Stanleyville (Kisangani). The UN helped to bring together a new national government and, in 1963, to end the Katanga secession. Later, Zaire faced several local rebellions and, in 1978, an invasion from Angola by (black) mercenary soldiers who had formerly served the Katanga regime; at Zaire's request, French and Belgian troops were sent in to repel these invaders.

The Zaire–Zambia frontier took its odd shape in the 1890s, when whites coming from South Africa met other whites, working for the 'Congo Free State' enterprise headed by King Leopold II of Belgium, who were moving south-eastwards. They drew a dividing line across a region rich in copper (*5*). At first the area south of the line was taken over by the British South Africa Company, created by the South African millionaire, Cecil Rhodes. Southern Rhodesia later became a 'self-governing' (in fact white-ruled) British colony, while Northern Rhodesia and Nyasaland were British protectorates. A federation of these three territories was formed in 1953 but dissolved in 1963 (*31*). In 1964 Northern Rhodesia and Nyasaland became independent as Zambia and Malawi. But Southern Rhodesia's whites refused to let power pass to the blacks who made up 95% of its population.

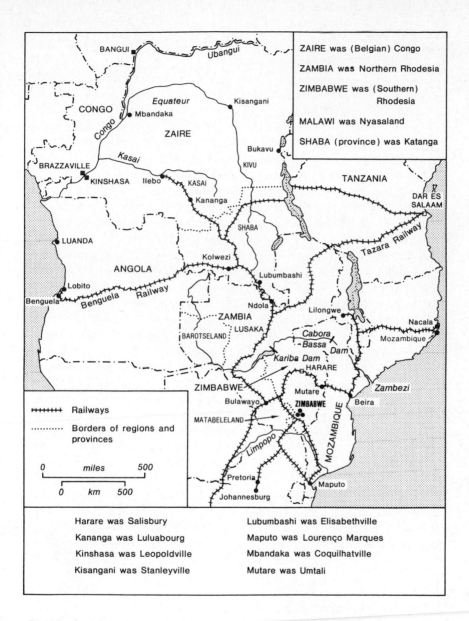

ZAIRE was (Belgian) Congo
ZAMBIA was Northern Rhodesia
ZIMBABWE was (Southern) Rhodesia
MALAWI was Nyasaland
SHABA (province) was Katanga

++++++ Railways

.... Borders of regions and provinces

0   miles   500

0   km   500

Harare was Salisbury
Kananga was Luluabourg
Kinshasa was Leopoldville
Kisangani was Stanleyville

Lubumbashi was Elisabethville
Maputo was Lourenço Marques
Mbandaka was Coquilhatville
Mutare was Umtali

In 1965 the whites proclaimed an independent republic.

Through the UN, British got trade embargoes ('sanctions') imposed on the rebel regime in Salisbury (now Harare), but South Africa helped it to withstand international pressures, and to resist the African guerrillas who

95

operated from bases in Zambia and, after 1975, in Mozambique. Rhodesian forces raided into those two states.

During the 1970s the strain on the Salisbury regime increased, and it was obliged to negotiate. In 1980, after a cease-fire, achieved through talks in London, an election held under British and Commonwealth supervision produced a new black government for what was now called Zimbabwe (from the site of ancient ruins in the south-east of the country). With sanctions ended and its independence recognized, Zimbabwe encouraged its whites to stay (although many moved to South Africa); but it now faced a resurgence of the old antagonism between its two main tribal groups, the Mashona majority and the formerly dominant Matabele (about 20% of the population). Unrest in Matabeleland led to harsh repression there in the mid-1980s.

In Mozambique, when Portugal withdrew in 1975, power passed to a leftist organization, Frelimo, which installed a one-party regime. Guerrilla resistance was soon launched by Renamo, a group which at first was more or less openly supported by South Africa. Although South African support was formally ended, and at least scaled down, in the 1980s, Renamo still held much of the interior of Mozambique in 1990 and had cut the railway lines from Maputo to Zimbabwe and from Beira to Malawi; the Beira–Zimbabwe line was operating, most of the time, only because Zimbabwe had sent troops to guard it (and the oil pipeline that runs near by). While other African governments were urging the Mozambique one to come to terms with Renamo, the combination of civil war, drought and mismanagement of the economy had devastated the country and inflicted famine on large areas.

33 South Africa

South Africa's population of about 37.5 million includes 5 million whites, three-fifths of whom are 'Afrikaners' (mostly of Dutch origin, speaking Afrikaans, a variant of Dutch), the others being English-speakers and mostly of British origin. There are 28 million black Africans; about a million Indians (although immigration from India has long been halted); and 3.2 million 'Coloureds', of mixed origin: paradoxically, in this country where race segregation was for many years imposed more strictly than anywhere else, past interbreeding has created a community of mixed origin which, in proportion to the white population, is uniquely large.

The first Dutch colony at Cape Town was established in 1652. Britain annexed the Cape of Good Hope in 1814. From then on, South Africa's history comprised two long struggles: between the British and the 'Boers', and between whites and blacks. From the 1860s onward the discoveries of diamonds, gold and other minerals, especially the gold of the Rand (Witwatersrand) around Johannesburg, increased the value of the prize. In the late 1940s the Afrikaners emerged as victors in both contests – for the time being.

From the 1950s onward, while white colonial rule was coming to an end elsewhere in Africa, a system of repression designed to perpetuate white minority rule was steadily tightened in South Africa. In 1961 the country became a republic and withdrew from the Commonwealth. During the 1960s Britain gave independence to the three adjacent protectorates, Basutoland (now Lesotho), Bechuanaland (now Botswana) and Swaziland, which South Africa had once expected to take over; but their economies remained dependent on the republic, and the change did not affect it much.

Between 1975 and 1980, however, South Africa lost the sheltering northern screen that had been provided by Portugal's colonies and by white-ruled Southern Rhodesia (*31, 32*). Its rulers were increasingly obliged to recognize their isolated international position. Britain, formerly South Africa's chief trading partner, imposed some economic 'sanctions' and was urged by other Commonwealth states to impose more; in 1986 the United States also imposed sanctions. Banks stopped providing credit; big international firms abandoned their South African operations. American pressure helped to bring about South Africa's withdrawal from Namibia (*34*).

Since the late 1950s great efforts had been made to abolish the country's black majority. Previously, blacks had been barred from owning any land except in small 'native reserves' (the Land Acts forced most blacks to find white employers, ensuring ample cheap labour for the white-owned farms and mines). The reserves were converted into 'homelands' ('Bantustans'), one for each of the main tribal groups, which were given a degree of self-government and urged to claim full independence. When a tribe's homeland became independent, all members of that tribe could be treated as 'foreign natives' – an almost unbelievable paradox – even though most of them had lived all their lives in 'white areas'. Thus South Africa would become a mainly white nation that happened to employ millions of black 'immigrants', who, of course, would have no political rights. By 1982 Bophuthatswana, Ciskei, Transkei and Venda had been declared independent while in practice remaining wholly dependent on South Africa, and 3.5 million blacks had been expelled from 'white' areas and dumped into the homelands, where there was neither work nor land for them.

In 1983 a new constitution provided for separate parliamentary chambers to be elected by the Indian and Coloured communities, who, it was hoped, would welcome this representation and not complain about the blacks still having none – while effective power would remain firmly in white hands. But most Coloureds and Indians refused to vote in the subsequent election. Some of them joined blacks in organizing protests against the constitution, which released more general unrest. The government had to impose a state of emergency, at first locally and then, in 1986, on a nation-wide scale.

In 1989 a new president, Frederik de Klerk, took a new course. By the end of 1990 he had lifted the state of emergency, lifted the ban on the African National Congress, released Nelson Mandela, Walter Sisulu and other long-detained ANC leaders, and proposed to hold talks with them about a drastic revision of the constitution. The ANC had announced a cease-fire in the (never extensive) guerrilla activity it had launched after being outlawed in 1961. But the signs were not all hopeful. Diehard Afrikaners were accusing their president of treachery to the traditions of the 'Volk'. The Pan-Africanist Congress denounced the ANC for giving up the 'armed struggle'. And in many black townships ANC supporters were embroiled in violent clashes with Zulu members of a rival organization, Inkatha. Its leader, Mangosuthu Buthelezi, chief minister of the Kwazulu homeland, had turned Inkatha, formerly a strictly Zulu group, into a poli-

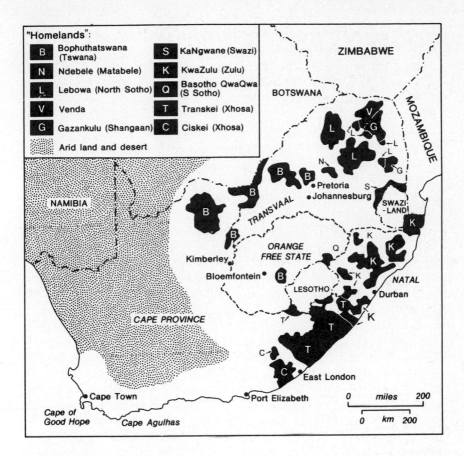

"Homelands":

B	Bophuthatswana (Tswana)	**S**	KaNgwane (Swazi)
N	Ndebele (Matabele)	**K**	KwaZulu (Zulu)
L	Lebowa (North Sotho)	**Q**	Basotho QwaQwa (S Sotho)
V	Venda	**T**	Transkei (Xhosa)
G	Gazankulu (Shangaan)	**C**	Ciskei (Xhosa)

Arid land and desert

tical party which, like the ANC, would be black-based but open to all races. Some ANC leaders saw his actions as intended to split the blacks and strengthen the government's hand; for his part, he was suspicious of the ANC's links with the communist party.

34 Angola and Namibia

In 1975 Portugal's withdrawal from Angola (*27, 31*) left three rival guerrilla movements fighting for power: in the north, the FNLA, based on the Bakongo tribes; in the south, UNITA, based on the Ovimbundu; and the leftist MPLA. South Africa sent a force to help UNITA, but the USSR flew Cuban troops in to help the MPLA, which was then able to hold the capital, Luanda. During the 1980s, while the FNLA lost importance, resistance to the MPLA regime was continued by UNITA. At the same time the Namibian guerrilla movement, SWAPO, was operating from Angola. To counter it, South Africa deployed large forces in northern Namibia (including the 'Caprivi Strip', named after the minister who got it included in what, from 1884 to 1914, was German South West Africa) and repeatedly occupied parts of southern Angola.

Namibia, taken over by South Africa after the 1914–18 war, is largely desert and has only 1.5 million inhabitants (including 80,000 whites); half of them are Ovambo, living in the north. Its most notable resources are the uranium mined at Rössing and the diamonds found south of Lüderitz. South Africa, which had held Namibia under a League of Nations mandate, refused to place it under UN trusteeship and rebuffed UN demands. (South Africa also maintained that Walvis Bay, the main port, was legally part of its Cape Province.)

In the late 1980s Angola's MPLA regime received less Soviet support and got most of its revenue from US oil firms. After long US mediation Angola, Cuba and South Africa signed agreements in 1988 under which, by 1991, the Cuban forces would have left Angola, while, in Namibia (*31*), the UN plan for a transition to independence would go ahead; accordingly, South African forces withdrew, a UN peacekeeping force took over temporarily, an election was held, and in 1990 Namibia became independent with a SWAPO-based government but a legal opposition in the legislature.

Although fighting continued in Angola in 1990, the government in Luanda had lost its 50,000-strong Cuban army, and the UNITA forces no longer had the help of Namibia-based South African troops. With encouragement from America, Portugal, Zaire and elsewhere, the two sides had held several rounds of peace talks.

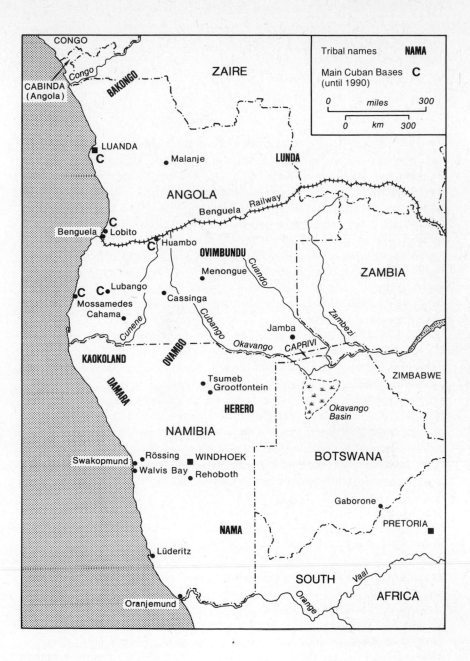

CONGO

CABINDA
(Angola)

ZAIRE

BAKONGO

Tribal names **NAMA**

Main Cuban Bases **C**
(until 1990)

0   miles   300

0   km   300

LUANDA
C

Malanje

LUNDA

ANGOLA

Benguela   Railway

Benguela **C**
Benguela ●Lobito

C Huambo

OVIMBUNDU

Menongue

Cuando

ZAMBIA

C **C**●Lubango
Mossamedes
Cahama ●

Cassinga

Cubango

Jamba

Zambezi

Cunene

Okavango   **CAPRIVI**

KAOKOLAND **OVAMBO**

ZIMBABWE

DAMARA

Tsumeb
●Grootfontein

Okavango
Basin

HERERO

NAMIBIA

Rössing
Swakopmund● ■ WINDHOEK
●Walvis Bay ●Rehoboth

BOTSWANA

Gaborone ●

PRETORIA ■

NAMA

Lüderitz ●

SOUTH

Vaal

Oranjemund ●

Orange

AFRICA

35 East Africa

Ethiopia (formerly called Abyssinia) was conquered by Fascist Italy in 1936 but liberated by British forces in 1941, re-emerging as Africa's only independent monarchy. Eritrea, a former Italian colony, was federated with Ethiopia in 1952. In 1962 Ethiopia imposed direct rule there, igniting Eritrean resistance. During the 1970s large parts of Eritrea fell into the guerrillas' hands, and a similar 'people's liberation front' began a rebellion in the neighbouring Tigre province.

After a military coup in 1974 Ethiopia became a Soviet sphere of influence. Its new rulers were army officers bent on transforming a country traditionally ruled by its emperor and its feudal chiefs and endowed with a distinctive Christian church (although many of its inhabitants, outside the central Amharic-speaking region, were Muslim).

The former Italian Somaliland (a UN trust territory from 1946 to 1960) and the former British Somaliland (the region around Berbera) were united in 1960 as an independent Somalia. Nationalist stirrings among the Muslim Somalis living in eastern Kenya, in the Haud and Ogaden regions of Ethiopia, and in Djibouti (then a French territory) led to many frontier clashes. An agreement in 1968 ended the Kenya-Somalia clashes. Dijbouti became independent in 1977, after the leaders of its Issa (Somali) and Afar communities had agreed to share power, but France retained a base there (*41*). Meanwhile the feud with Ethiopia had led Somalia to sign a pact with the USSR and permit Soviet bases to be built on its soil.

In 1977 the Ogaden Somalis rebelled, Somalia sent troops to support them, and a full-scale war ensued, which the Ethiopians won because the USSR took their side, flying in 20,000 Cuban soldiers as well as arms. From then on the USSR provided arms and advisers for Ethiopian forces fighting in Eritrea and Tigre as well as for those on the Somalia frontier. Somalia expelled the Soviet military missions and began to look to the Americans for support. Not until 1988 were Somalia and Ethiopia able to agree to restore relations, exchange prisoners of war and disengage their forces in the frontier zone. Then northern (ex-British) Somalia erupted in a rebellion which by 1990 had spread across most of the country. Over a million Somalis, fleeing from all these conflicts, were by then in refugee camps on both sides of the Ethiopia frontier.

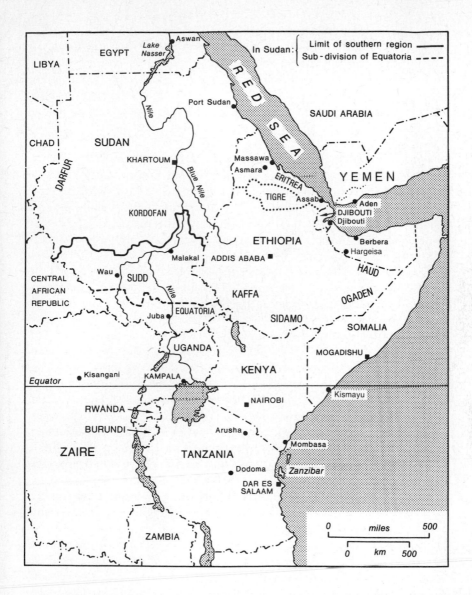

Map legend:
In Sudan: Limit of southern region ——
Sub-division of Equatoria - - - -

LIBYA
EGYPT
Lake Nasser
Aswan
Port Sudan
RED SEA
SAUDI ARABIA
CHAD
SUDAN
DARFUR
KHARTOUM
Blue Nile
Nile
Massawa
Asmara
ERITREA
YEMEN
TIGRE
Assab
Aden
DJIBOUTI
Djibouti
KORDOFAN
ETHIOPIA
Berbera
Hargeisa
HAUD
Malakal
ADDIS ABABA
CENTRAL AFRICAN REPUBLIC
Wau
SUDD
Nile
KAFFA
OGADEN
EQUATORIA
Juba
SIDAMO
SOMALIA
UGANDA
MOGADISHU
Equator
Kisangani
KAMPALA
KENYA
NAIROBI
Kismayu
RWANDA
BURUNDI
Arusha
Mombasa
ZAIRE
TANZANIA
Dodoma
Zanzibar
DAR ES SALAAM
ZAMBIA

0   miles   500
0   km   500

Meanwhile the Ethiopian army (still Soviet-equipped but no longer stiffened by the Cuban troops, who had gone home) was losing ground on its northern fronts. In 1990 the Eritreans captured the key port of Massawa and encircled Asmara; the Tigreans had pushed far south on the road to the capital, Addis Ababa; the government was obliged to start talks with the guerrilla leaders. Famine had become a recurrent threat in a region where the fighting obstructed international efforts to bring in relief food during droughts (*30*). Many refugees had crossed into Sudan. (In 1984 about 20,000 Falashas – Ethiopian Jews – had got across the border into Sudan, whence they were flown to Israel. In 1990 the Ethiopian regime was haggling with Israel, demanding arms in return for letting more Falashas leave.)

Sudan, formerly an Anglo-Egyptian condominium (in practice ruled by the British), became independent in 1956. From then on its black south was in revolt against the dominance of the Arabized Muslim north almost continuously until 1972, when the south was granted regional autonomy. In 1983 a new southern rebellion began when the government in Khartoum threatened to impose Islamic (*sharia*) laws all over Sudan. Ethiopia backed the rebels. As in Ethiopia, civil war compounded famine. In 1990 Sudan seemed close to disintegration. Its military rulers had run it into bankruptcy, lost all the south except a few towns supplied only by air, given Libya a free hand in the western province of Darfur (*37*) and alienated Saudi Arabia and other formerly friendly Arab states, including Egypt, by applauding Iraq's invasion of Kuwait (*45*).

Kenya, Uganda, Tanganyika and Zanzibar (the last two being united in 1964 as Tanzania) had all been British-ruled before they came to independence in the 1960s (*9*). For a time they went on operating transport and other services jointly, but by 1977 their East African Community had collapsed; Kenya and Tanzania were on such bad terms that the frontier between them was closed until 1983. The worst troubles, however, developed in Uganda.

Uganda had become independent with a constitution that preserved its tribal monarchies. In 1967 President Obote abolished the monarchies; by this and other arbitrary actions he aroused much opposition, especially among the Baganda, the people of the old kingdom of Buganda. The army commander, General Amin, seized power in 1971, imposed a reign of terror, expelled the Asian community and, in 1976, collaborated with Arab and German hi-jackers who brought a planeload of hostages, including many Israelis, to Entebbe airport. (An Israeli airborne commando rescued the hostages.) In 1978 his forces invaded Tanzania. Counter-attacking, the Tanzanians met little resistance, although Libya sent troops to help Amin's, which fled into Zaire and Sudan. Obote, whom the Tanzanians favoured, was soon back in power, but his soldiers proved as brutal as Amin's, provoking a guerrilla resistance movement, which in 1986 captured Kampala and formed a new government.

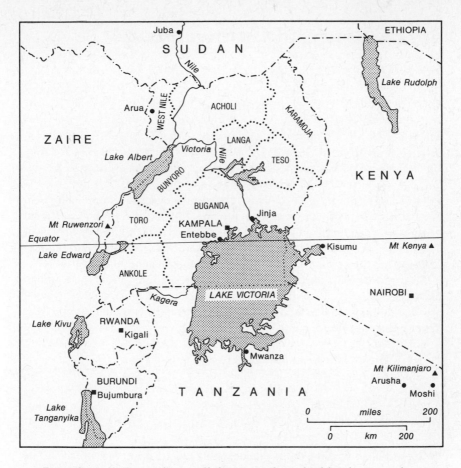

Rwanda and Burundi, small but populous highland states, became independent in 1962, after periods of German and then (under UN trusteeship) Belgian rule. About 15% of Burundi's inhabitants belong to the long dominant (and distinctively tall) Watutsi tribes; they control the army, which in 1972 and again in 1988 suppressed revolts among the majority Hutu (Bahutu) tribes. In Rwanda similar Watutsi dominance was overthrown in 1959; many Watutsi fled into Uganda. In 1990 Rwanda was invaded from Uganda by a force, recruited from these Watutsi exiles, which outnumbered Rwanda's small army. At Rwanda's request, Belgian, French and Zairean troops were sent to help protect the capital, Kigali. Uganda denied responsibility for the invasion, but some of Rwanda's leaders said they suspected that both Uganda and Libya (*38*) had helped to launch it.

36 Nigeria and Guinea coast

Around the Gulf of Guinea five European nations' colonial rivalries left a patchwork of frontiers. Until 1957 the region's only sovereign state was Liberia, where American-sponsored settlement of freed slaves had begun in the 1820s; but by 1975 all the colonies had become independent.

Germany's two pre-1914 colonies, Togo and Cameroon, were later each divided into British and French territories. In 1960 the French portions became independent states and, after UN-supervised plebiscites, British Togoland joined Ghana; the British Cameroons' northern part joined Nigeria, and the southern part joined (ex-French) Cameroun.

Several attempts to unite the small new states failed. In 1981 the Gambia (British until 1965) called in troops from (ex-French) Senegal to help suppress an attempted coup, and the two states formed a confederation, called Senegambia; but this remained only a loose link throughout the 1980s. The

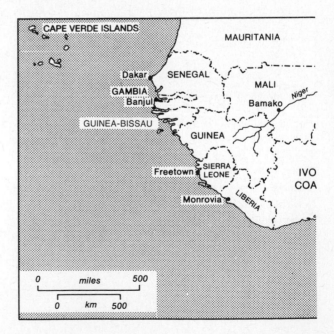

Cape Verde Islands and Guinea-Bissau, both former Portuguese colonies, abandoned their plans to unite in 1980.

After independence many new names appeared. The Gold Coast became Ghana; (ex-French) Soudan became Mali; French, Portuguese and Spanish Guinea became respectively Guinea, Guinea-Bissau and Equatorial Guinea. In 1975 Dahomey renamed itself Benin (although Benin City is in Nigeria). The Gambian capital, Bathurst, became Banjul; Chad's capital, Fort Lamy, became Ndjamena. After a military coup in 1983 Upper Volta was renamed Burkina Faso. In 1985 it fought a short war with Mali over a disputed border area south-east of Timbuktu, the 'Agacher strip'; the rival claims were then submitted to the International Court at The Hague.

Friction between Senegal and Mauritania led in 1989 first to frontier clashes and then to race riots in both countries; hundreds of people were killed, hundreds of thousands fled across the frontier in both directions. This is a racial, not a religious, problem: both countries are Muslim, but most Senegalese are black, most Mauritanians fair-skinned, and although Mauritania has repeatedly announced the abolition of its ancient custom of keeping black slaves the announcements have had little practical effect.

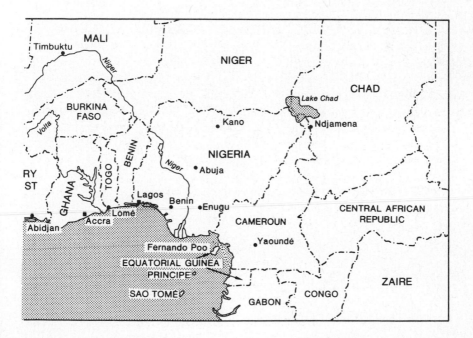

West Africa's religious dividing line is more widely significant. It is Islamic north of a line from Senegal to northern Nigeria, Christian or animist to the south. The division has caused much difficulty in Nigeria, Africa's most populous country, which overshadows all its neighbours. In 1960 Nigeria became independent as a federation, with a huge Muslim northern region and two smaller ones, the western dominated by the Yoruba people, the eastern by the Ibo. After two military coups some Ibo leaders proclaimed in 1967 at Enugu a secessionist state, called Biafra. They were not subdued until 1970. This civil war brought mass starvation to the Ibo region and bitter dissension among African governments, several of which supported Biafra.

Nigeria was reshaped as a federation of 19 states, Abuja was chosen to succeed Lagos as the capital, and from 1979 to 1983 a new attempt was made to maintain an elected civilian government. Then Nigeria's oil boom collapsed, the 2 million immigrants whom the boom had drawn in were brusquely ordered to go home (to Ghana, for many of them) and military rule was imposed again. Increasingly the military regime brought domination by Muslim northerners. In 1989-90 resentful southerners hatched several coup plots, which failed and were followed by many secret trials and executions.

Nigeria, Niger and the 14 other states to the west of them are members of the Economic Community of West African States (ECOWAS), founded in 1975. The members agreed in 1990 to send a peacekeeping force (mainly Nigerian, but also from the Gambia, Ghana, Guinea and Sierra Leone) to try to stop the civil war in Liberia, which had devastated the country and was rapidly destroying its capital, Monrovia. Four months later, at a West African 'summit' conference held at Bamako, the three warring Liberian forces were induced to agree to a cease-fire. This was a striking exception to the general rule of non-intervention in the region's many civil wars and internal upheavals. Since gaining independence, Benin, Burkina Faso, Ghana, Guinea, Guinea-Bissau, Mali, Mauritania, Niger, Nigeria, Sierra Leone and Togo had all undergone coups, and Liberia itself had previously, in 1980, had a notoriously bloody one.

37 Ex-French Africa

France's former territories in north and west Africa formed a continuous area stretching from the Mediterranean to the Congo river (*27 32*). In this area there are now 17 sovereign states. In the north, Morocco, Algeria and Tunisia are Arab countries (*29, 38*). The other 14 states, formerly grouped as French West and French Equatorial Africa, have a combined population much smaller than Nigeria's; the Sahara desert covers most of Mauritania and much of Mali, Niger and Chad.

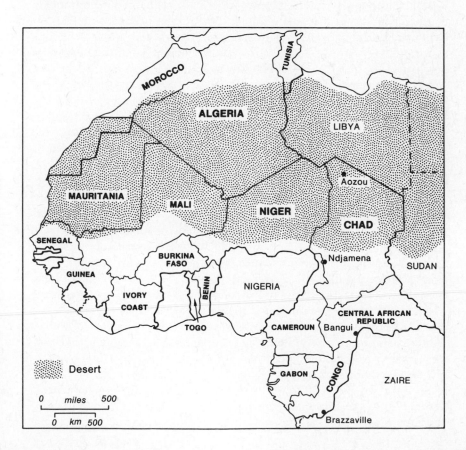

Guinea became independent in 1958, the other 13 in 1960. Congo has often been called Congo-Brazzaville, to distinguish it from the former Belgian Congo, now Zaire. The Central African Republic was declared an 'empire' in 1976 by its ruler, Colonel Bokassa, but he was ousted in 1979 and the CAR resumed its claim to be a republic. Mauritania's iron ore, Guinea's bauxite, Gabon's oil and Niger's uranium (*3–5*, *39*) are notable resources in a region otherwise poorly endowed, and much afflicted by drought in the 'Sahel' belt along the Sahara's southern edge (*30*). French aid has been important to most of the 14 states; France retained the right to use bases in the CAR, Chad, Gabon, Ivory Coast and Senegal. Some states, including Benin, Congo and Guinea, have at times accepted Soviet influence. But during the 1970s Libya's ambitions became the most disturbing factor in the region (*38*).

Libya's most open intervention was in Chad. In 1973, taking advantage of Chad's recurrent factional fighting, the Libyans occupied the 'Aozou strip', where they hoped to find uranium deposits like those in neighbouring Niger. In 1980 they sent troops to Ndjamena, and in 1981 they proclaimed the union of Chad with Libya. The OAU (*30*) pressed them to withdraw, and they did so; but in 1982 they established at Bardai, near Aozou, a 'government of national unity' (GUNT) consisting of dissident Chadian faction leaders. (In protest, so many African presidents refused to attend the OAU 'summit' due to be held in Libya in 1982 that it was never held.) In 1983 the Libyans captured Faya Largeau, an oasis town. France sent a force to Chad; it was withdrawn in 1984, but Libya and its GUNT clients failed to take over any areas except the desert region in northern Chad, and the GUNT group disintegrated. In 1987 Chad's forces, although lightly armed and facing Libya's Soviet-built tanks and aircraft, recaptured Faya Largeau and drove the Libyans back into the Aozou area. OAU mediation brought a cease-fire. Libya's prestige was badly impaired.

In 1989 the Chad regime, in turn, began to disintegrate. Some army chiefs retreated, with their troops, into Sudan (which by then had little control of its western Darfur province, *35*); and in 1990 they re-entered Chad, meeting little resistance and rapidly taking over the capital, Ndjamena. The ousted regime's leaders asked for French help, but France refused, pointing out that although the new victors had obtained arms from Libya they were not Libyan puppets.

Libya had, however, started to meddle actively in Sudan's now chaotic affairs (*35*). In the small states of 'black Africa', south of the Sahara, Colonel Qaddafi's Libyan regime already had a long record of meddling and attempts to gain ascendancy. Libyan diplomats had been caught

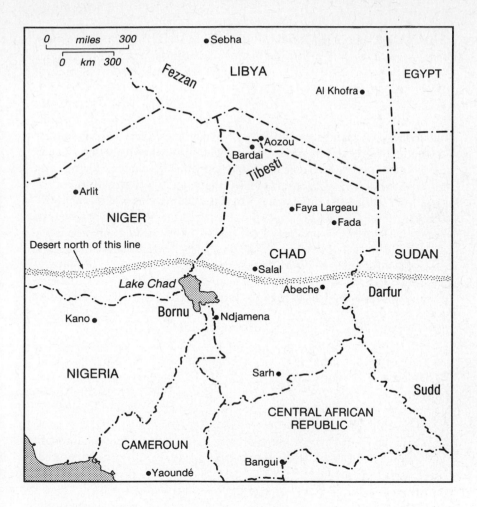

smuggling explosives into Senegal, and had been involved in coup plots in Benin, Gambia and Sierra Leone. A 1983 coup in Burkina Faso had installed a regime that accepted Libyan subsidies. (Libya's huge oil revenues were also widely used to subsidise opposition groups and terrorists in various countries.)

38 North Africa

In the Maghreb (the 'West' of the Arab world), two former French protec-torates, Morocco and Tunisia, became independent in 1956, but Algeria did not achieve independence until 1962, after seven years of fighting. The political turmoil in France caused by that long conflict was ended by President Charles de Gaulle, who defied and outmanoeuvred the powerful 'French Algeria' interests – and escaped the assassination with which he was threatened when he ordered the army to withdraw from Algeria. Since France first colonized it in 1830 a million Europeans had settled in Algeria; nearly all of them left after 1962. A large-scale migration to France of Algerians and other North Africans also developed (23). These Muslim populations' growth rates were high, and the fertile land area is limited by

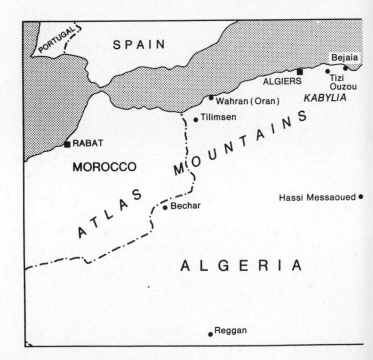

the Atlas mountains and, to the south, by the Sahara desert (*1*).

These countries' main culture is Arabic (with French elements super-imposed), but the original Berber population's language and customs survive in many places in Algeria and Morocco – notably in Kabylia, east of Algiers, where demands for the protection of Berber culture were mounted in the 1970s and 1980s. Both Arabs and Berbers are Muslim, and Morocco's kings have for centuries been religious leaders as well as rulers. The post-independence regimes in Algeria and Tunisia were secular in character, but Islamic fundamentalist groups (*28*) grew rapidly in the 1980s. In Algerian local elections in 1990 one such party won 55% of the votes; the turnout was low, especially in Berber areas (and husbands cast votes for their wives), but the fundamentalists evidently hoped to take over the government within a year or two.

In 1989 the Arab Maghreb Union (AMU) was formed by Algeria, Libya, Mauritania (*37*), Morocco and Tunisia. One of their aims was to combine in dealings with the European Community (*19*), with which almost two-thirds of their foreign trade was done, and where more than 3 million

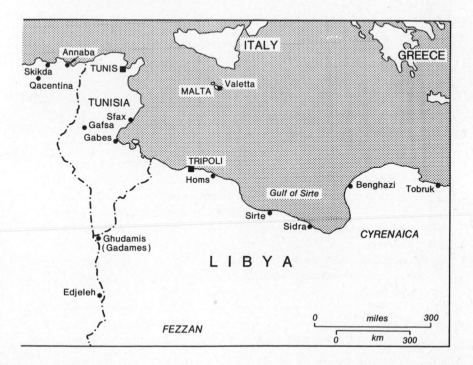

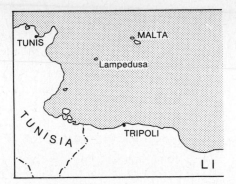

Maghrebis were working (about a million of them having got into jobs illegally). They feared that, with Greece, Portugal and Spain now inside the EC, these rival producers of citrus fruit and olive oil would deprive them of export sales, and that the flow of labour from those countries to France and Italy would mean fewer job openings there for North Africans.

The forming of the AMU marked a putting aside of many old quarrels. Algeria and Morocco had fought over disputed frontier lines in the 1960s, and became even more antagonistic after 1975, when Algeria was the host and main backer of the Polisario guerrillas who were trying to evict the Moroccans from Western Sahara (*39*). In 1987 Algeria and Morocco exchanged prisoners-of-war; in 1988 they resumed diplomatic relations after a 12-year break; in 1989 came the AMU pact. But Algeria's enthusiasm for fighting a 'proxy war' with Morocco, through the Polisario, had been waning for some time. The real surprise in 1989 was the drawing of Libya into a grouping which it could not hope to dominate, and with whose other members it had often picked quarrels.

Libya had become independent in 1951 – having been taken from Turkey by Italy in 1911, fought over by the British, Italians and Germans in the 1939–45 war, and then, for a few years, administered by the British and (in the southern Fezzan region) the French. It has only 3.75 million inhabitants and is mostly desert, but in the 1960s it was spectacularly enriched by new-found oilfields. In 1969 Colonel Moamer Qaddafi and other officers seized power and launched ambitious foreign policies, using the huge oil revenues, terrorist techniques and their own brand of 'Islamic' slogans.

Libyan forces were sent to fight, unsuccessfully, in Uganda (*35*) and Chad (*37*). Libya financed and supported attempts to destabilize and overthrow governments in a dozen Arab and African states, and its agents carried out or attempted assassinations in those states, in several European

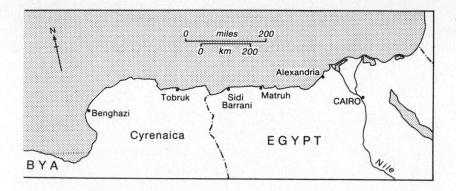

countries, and in the United States. In 1980 Qaddafi proclaimed a policy of hunting down dissidents who had escaped from Libya; the killers were directed and armed through Libyan 'diplomatic missions'. In 1984, after a series of murders in Britain, machine-gun fire from the mission in London wounded 12 demonstrators and killed a policewoman. When a country (e.g. Germany in 1983, Italy in 1986) caught a Libyan gunman, Libya would take foreigners hostage to enforce his release. Qaddafi also armed and financed German, Indonesian, Irish, Palestinian and other terrorist groups; in a 1989 interview he admitted having helped terrorists but claimed he had stopped.

Qaddafi made a habit of proclaiming 'unions' with other countries: e.g. with Syria in 1980, with Chad in 1981 (*37*), with Morocco in 1984, with Sudan in 1990. He always wanted Libya to be the dominant partner, and the 'unions' never got far. His sea claims also caused tension; in 1980 his warships forced Malta to stop exploring for oil 60 miles from its coast, and in 1981 and 1986 his aircraft attacked US ones over the Gulf of Sirte, which Libya claimed as 'internal waters'. Also in 1986 the US held Libya responsible for the killing of US soldiers in Berlin, and in reprisal US aircraft bombed Tripoli and Benghazi. Other cases in which suspicions were directed at Libya included: the 1984 laying of mines which damaged 17 ships in the Red Sea (*45*); the 1988 Lockerbie disaster, in which a bomb destroyed a US airliner over Scotland; and, in 1988–90, the discovery at Rabta, 50 miles south of Tripoli, of a heavily guarded 'pharmaceuticals' plant, built with German help, which seemed likely to produce poison gas.

39 Morocco and Western Sahara

Before Morocco became independent in 1956 most of it had been under French control, but Spain had held zones in the north and south, and Tangier had been an international zone. Until 1969 Spain retained an enclave at Ifni, and it still holds Ceuta and Melilla (25).

In 1975 Spain withdrew from its Western Sahara territory – a very thinly peopled, mainly desert area, its only notable resources being the phosphates near Bou Craa. Morocco, which had old claims to the territory, sent in troops, while Mauritania took over part of the southern region (Rio de Oro). They both met resistance from the Polisario guerrilla movement, backed by Algeria and based on the Tindouf area. In 1979 Mauritania withdrew its forces. Morocco then took over positions in the south, but could not stop the guerrillas operating in the desert interior there, which they could reach from Tindouf by crossing Mauritania's desert areas. Between 1980 and 1989 the Moroccans built a long chain of sand 'walls', gradually extended southward until they protected the whole territory except for some desert border stretches. Before the completion of the southernmost walls, Polisario attacks shifted to the south, alarming Mauritania, which feared that the fighting might damage the rail and road links between its iron ore mines and the coast.

Morocco had offered to hold a referendum so that the Sahrawis (Saharans) could choose between independence and attachment to Morocco. But there were many disputes about who should be entitled to vote: before 1975 about half the Saharans were nomads who moved in and out of the territory each year; now many of them were living in Polisario-controlled refugee camps around Tindouf, and there had been some migration south from Morocco. By 1984 a majority of African governments had recognized the government-in-exile which the Polisario leaders had proclaimed. When its delegates were seated at meetings of the Organization for Africa Unity (OAU), Morocco withdrew in protest (30).

However, Mauritania restored relations with Morocco in 1985, while continuing to recognize the 'Saharan Arab Democratic Republic' (SADR). By 1990 Libya and, more important, Algeria had stopped giving the Polisario arms and encouragement. There was still no agreement on the terms of a referendum, but the improvement of relations among the Arab govern-

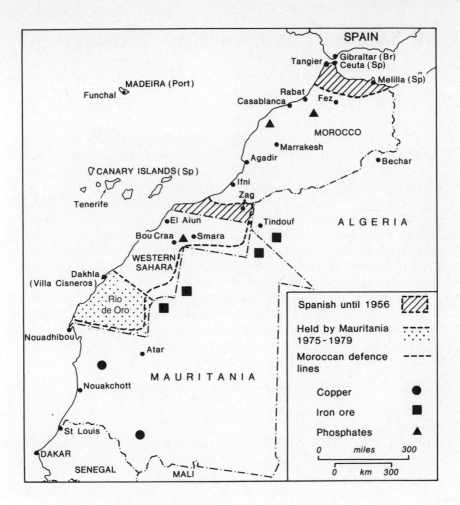

ments of the Maghreb (*29, 38*) seemed to have left the Polisario without any real backing. Its leaders were quarrelling and some of them had switched to the Moroccan side.

40 Middle East and North African oil

Oil production began in Iran (Persia) in 1912; in northern Iraq, around Kirkuk, in the 1920s; in Saudia Arabia in 1939; in Kuwait in 1945. By the mid-1950s the Middle East was producing a fifth of the world's oil, and supplying three-quarters of western Europe's needs. The Arab countries of North Africa then began to produce oil (and Algeria also developed a big export trade in natural gas). In 1960 the Middle East and North African oil-exporting states – all of them Arab, except Iran – were producing a quarter of the world's output; by 1970 they were producing two-fifths of it. Much of this oil came from desert areas, and the wealth it brought transformed the position of such countries as Saudi Arabia and Libya.

The oilfields were originally developed by western companies – American, British, Dutch and French in Iraq, American and British in Kuwait, American in Saudi Arabia. In 1951 the British company working in Iran was expropriated and its refinery at Abadan was seized. Thereafter the

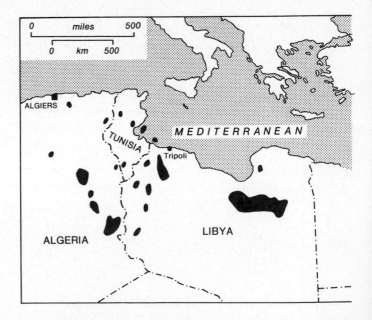

exporting states took an increasingly tight grip on the industry, raising taxes, nationalizing some firms, setting stiffer terms for others and creating their own state oil corporations. But the region's oil, being plentiful and accessible (even the offshore fields in the Gulf are in relatively shallow water), remained cheap enough to take a growing share of the world market.

Pipelines were built to carry some Iraqi and Saudi oil to ports on the Mediterranean but most oil from the Gulf region went by tanker from Gulf ports even before the flow through the pipelines was affected by successive conflicts involving Syria, Lebanon and Israel. Tankers bound for Europe mostly used the Suez Canal until it, too, was affected by the region's conflicts; but when it was closed in 1967 (42) the longer 'Cape route' around South Africa had to be used, and bigger tankers were built. The oil traffic did not all return to the Suez Canal when it was reopened in 1975 and deepened and widened in 1980.

Meanwhile, alternative shortcuts emerged. When Israel opened a pipeline from Eilat to the Mediterranean in 1970 it could not expect Arab governments to approve of Arab oil passing through it; but in 1977 Egypt opened the 'Sumed' pipeline, running from south of Suez to a point on the Mediterranean near Alexandria. There are now also pipelines that carry

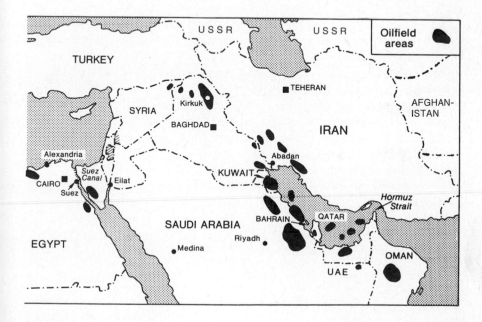

oil from Saudi Arabia and Iraq to Yanbu, a port near Medina, and oil from Iraq to the Mediterranean through Turkey.

Iraq, by its own action, deprived itself of the ability to ship oil out through the Gulf in 1980, when one of the first consequences of its invasion of Iran (48) was the blocking of all access by sea to its Basra port and oil terminals. In 1990, when international sanctions were imposed on Iraq after its occupation of Kuwait (45), the Saudis and Turks prevented Iraqi oil passing through the pipelines across their territory: thus Iraq could export no oil at all.

One reason for the sharp international reaction to the invasion of Kuwait in 1990 was that, of all known world reserves of oil, about 10% were in Kuwait, 10% in Iraq and 25% in Saudi Arabia. By seizing Kuwait the Iraqis increased their share of reserves to a fifth of the total. If the grabbing of Kuwait were to be tamely accepted the Iraqi rulers might feel that they could safely proceed to grab the adjacent Saudi oilfields – thus making themselves masters of 45% of the world's oil reserves.

The proximity of the USSR to the oil-rich Gulf region, with its vulnerably weak states and its local conflicts, had been arousing western fears, particularly after the Soviet occupation of Afghanistan in 1979 (49). The 1970s had already seen the withdrawal of the last British forces from the region, and the upheaval that ended Iran's role as a western-equipped buffer against possible Soviet southward thrusts (41, 47). In the 1980s, however, the Iran–Iraq war posed a much more immediate threat to the flow of oil from the Gulf (48); then in 1990 came the invasion of Kuwait. Westerners looking at the USSR tended to see it less as a threat to the unstable Middle East than as a potential source of help in moderating the instability.

By 1990, moreover, there was no longer any doubt about the drastic effects on the world economy that conflicts involving Middle East oil could produce. Saudi Arabia was the biggest producer, not only among members of the Organization of Arab Petroleum Exporting Countries (OAPEC), but also in the wider grouping, OPEC (3). Seven of OPEC's 12 other member states were also in the Middle East and North Africa. Although the OPEC group was not as dominant as it had been in the 1970s, the heavy dependence on Middle East oil of Japan, now an economic superpower, was one of the more conspicuous indications that any new Gulf conflict would have wide international repercussions.

41 Suez and Indian Ocean

The Suez Canal was built in the 1860s by a French-based international company, by agreement with the rulers of Egypt and of the Turkish empire, which then included Egypt, although its hold was uncertain. In 1882 the British occupied Egypt, completing a strategic chain in which the main links were Gibraltar, Malta, Suez and Aden. The Suez route had dramatically reduced the time that ships from Britain took to reach the Indian Ocean region and the Far East. It became Britain's main imperial 'lifeline' to its possessions in the east, which at one time included India, Burma, Malaya, Australia, New Zealand, much of East Africa and many islands in the Indian Ocean and the Pacific. The protection of this lifeline was a British preoccupation. Moreover, Britain later became dependent for three-quarters of its oil supplies on tankers from the Middle East passing through the Suez Canal (40); its own North Sea oilfields were not fully developed until the end of the 1970s.

When Egypt became independent in 1922 Britain retained control of the country's defence. Under the 1936 treaty British forces withdrew from most of Egypt but remained in the canal zone. In the 1939–45 war, when British and Commonwealth forces repelled German and Italian attempts to capture the canal and reach the Indian Ocean, the canal zone became a major British base. This base was finally evacuated, on Egyptian insistence, a few months before the 1956 Suez conflict (42).

Meanwhile the British relinquishment of empire had begun with the granting of independence to India and Pakistan in 1947. The process had almost been completed, 'east of Suez', by 1967 – when, as a result of the Six Day War (42), the canal was closed until 1975. In 1968 Britain announced plans to remove its remaining forces from the small Gulf states and Singapore (46, 62) by 1971. Among the Indian Ocean islands, Britain gave independence to the Maldives in 1965 (although they did not join the Commonwealth until 1982), to Mauritius in 1968 and to Seychelles in 1976 (when the islands of Aldabra, Desroches and Farquhar were transferred to Seychelles control).

With the era of British predominance in the Indian Ocean thus ended, the Suez Canal lost much of its strategic importance. However, the new situation in the region carried an echo of the nineteenth-century period when the British saw Russia's conquest of central Asia (53) as a threat to their Indian empire and feared that Russia would try to reach the Indian Ocean by way of Iran (then usually called Persia). Tsarist Russia had been deterred from trying to take control of Afghanistan, but the USSR was not (49). Although by 1989 Afghan resistance had forced the Soviet occupying army to withdraw, the USSR had established itself in the Indian Ocean some years earlier as a naval power. It was able to use bases that it had acquired on the coasts of Vietnam, Ethiopia and what was then South Yemen, whose communist rulers provided it with facilities both at Aden and at the island of Socotra (35, 45, 60).

By the 1980s the former Soviet bases in Somalia were available to the Americans, who were also maintaining a naval presence in the region and obtaining facilities in Oman (35, 45). Farther south, the Americans had built staging facilities on Diego Garcia island, in the Chagos group – officially, since 1965, the British Indian Ocean Territory (BIOT). This last remaining British dependency in the region had presented its own problems. In 1982 Britain agreed to pay compensation to the former plantation workers who had been moved from Diego Garcia to Mauritius between 1965 and 1973; meanwhile Mauritius put in a claim to the Chagos group.

Réunion remained an overseas *département* of France, which also had base facilities at Djibouti (35). France had granted independence to Madagascar in 1960 and to the Comoros in 1975, but the people of Mayotte, one of the Comoro islands, had insisted on retaining French protection, and Madagascar laid claim to several uninhabited islands on which France maintained weather stations (one of them, Tromelin, was also claimed by Mauritius).

During the 1980s the threat to Gulf shipping created by the Iran–Iraq war, the *rapprochement* between the superpowers, and then, in 1990, Iraq's aggression against Kuwait, all had the effect of turning the major powers' minds towards some degree of co-operation in the Indian Ocean region (7, 45, 48). Towards the end of 1990 there was even some debate in Japan about the possibility of Japanese forces joining in the UN-backed resistance to Iraq (one of the biggest elements in Indian Ocean traffic being the massive movement of Gulf oil to Japan).

The small island states in the Indian Ocean did not always, in the 1980s, preserve the image of a tranquil tropical paradise. In Seychelles the regime that had been installed by a coup in 1977 survived attempted counter-coups in 1981 and 1982, calling in troops from Tanzania to its aid. India sent forces to help the Maldives fight off a coup attempted in 1988 by Sri Lanka

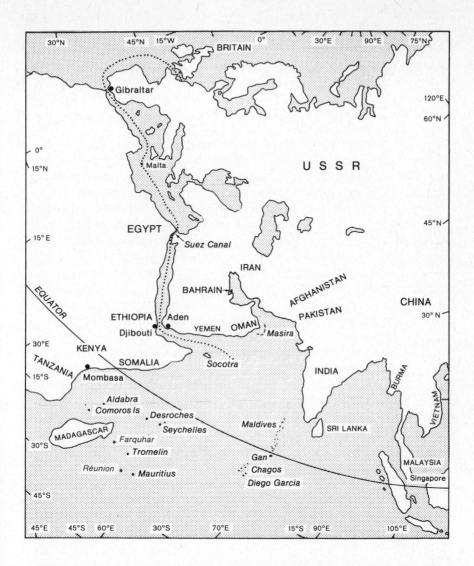

Tamil mercenaries hired by a rich Maldivian. In 1989 a French force went to the Comoros and removed a band of French and Belgian mercenaries who, with financial backing from South African sources, had more and more openly made themselves masters of the islands.

42 Israel and Arabs I

In an area formerly part of the Turkish empire, Syria and Lebanon were taken over by France, Palestine and Transjordan by Britain, after the 1914–1918 war – all under League of Nations mandates. The Palestine mandate provided for the creation of a Jewish 'national home', without damage to the existing population's interests – a difficult aim. Since the 1890s the Zionist movement had been promoting Jewish settlement in Palestine. Under the mandate Jewish immigration increased, especially when the persecution of Jews began in Nazi Germany (*18*), and Arab–Jewish hostility boiled up. After the Nazis' massacre of millions of Jews during the 1939–45 war, Zionism won wider support, particularly in America; survivors of the 'Holocaust' struggled to reach Palestine; the British, finding it hard to restrict Jewish entry and to curb the Arab–Jewish conflicts, took the problem to the United Nations in 1947. By then there were about 600,000 Jews, 1,100,000 Muslim Arabs and 150,000 (mainly Arab) Christians in Palestine.

The UN Assembly approved a plan (backed by both the USA and the USSR) to partition Palestine. The Arabs rejected it. In 1948 the British pulled out. The Jews proclaimed the new state of Israel, but it was attacked by all the neighbouring Arab countries, while fighting also continued between Palestinian Arabs and Jews.

When UN mediation secured armistices in 1949 the Israelis were left holding more territory than the partition plan would have given them. Transjordan (independent since 1946) annexed half of Jerusalem and the hilly regions of Samaria and Judaea (the 'West Bank'), renaming itself the Kingdom of Jordan. Egypt held the 'Gaza strip'. Most of the former Arab inhabitants of what was now Israel had become refugees in Gaza, Jordan and other Arab states. The Arab governments refused to make peace, or to recognize Israel, or to let its ships use the Suez Canal or the Gulf of Aqaba (*41*). Despite the efforts of UN observers on the frontiers, Arab raids and Israeli retaliations recurred.

In 1956 an international crisis developed when Egypt expropriated the Suez Canal Company and rebuffed the major canal-using countries' proposals for a new regime for the canal (*6, 41*). In October Israel attacked and defeated the Egyptian army in Sinai. When Israel's troops got close to the canal the British and French governments demanded to be allowed to

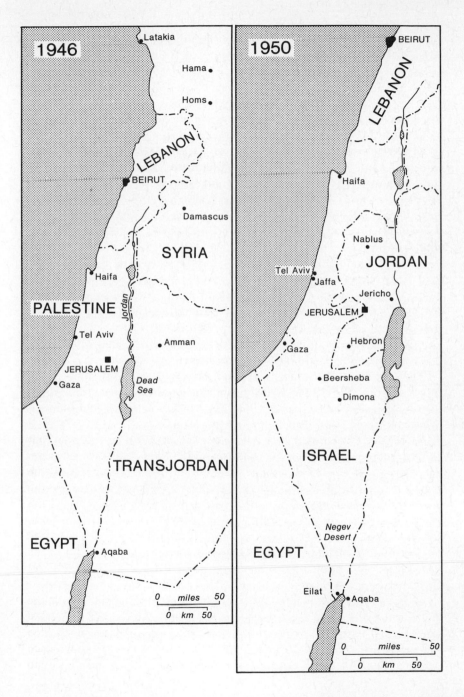

take control of it; they claimed that their aim was to protect the canal, but they also wanted to strike a blow at Egypt, which was then contesting their influence throughout the Arab world. The extent of their collusion with Israel became clear later. British bombing destroyed much of Egypt's air force on the ground. British and French troops captured Port Said and moved south along the canal. The UN Assembly called for British, French and Israeli withdrawal and approved the sending of an emergency force (UNEF). By April 1957 the British, French and Israeli forces had left Egypt, and the UN had cleared the canal (which Egypt had blocked by sinking ships in it). Egypt continued to bar Israeli vessels from the canal, but they could now use the Gulf of Aqaba, where a UNEF unit was posted at Sharm el Sheikh. UNEF successfully policed Israeli's border with Egypt until 1967, but raids and reprisals continued on its borders with Syria and Jordan.

In May 1967 Egypt moved a large army up to the Israel border, demanded UNEF's immediate removal and reoccupied Sharm el Sheikh, announcing a new blockade in the Gulf of Aqaba. Israel's appeals to the UN brought it no reassurance, and in June it attacked Egypt, Syria and Jordan. In this 'Six Day War' Israel captured the whole West Bank; Gaza and all of Sinai up to the canal; and the Golan heights, from which Syria had been able to bombard the Galilee lowlands.

The Suez Canal was now a 'front line', closed to all traffic (until 1975), but Israel could use the Gulf of Aqaba. Israel had acquired better defence lines (before 1967 even its biggest city, Tel Aviv, risked being shelled from the nearby hills held by Jordan), but it had also acquired territories – the West Bank and Gaza – that had large Arab populations. With all Palestine now in Israeli hands the Palestinian Arabs showed a stronger spirit of resistance. Rival exiles' guerrilla groups combined in the Palestine Liberation Organization (PLO) – although the rivalries remained, different Arab states backed different groups, and terrorist activity in western countries conflicted with the PLO's appeals for international sympathy. (In 1970 four western airliners were hi-jacked simultaneously; in 1972, at the Munich Olympics, 11 Israeli athletes were kidnapped and murdered.)

In 1970 the PLO forces in Jordan challenged its government's authority, were defeated by its army in large-scale fighting, and lost their bases there. The PLO then became mainly based in Lebanon, with head-quarters in Beirut. As a result it was Israel's northernmost settlements that were most persistently attacked in the 1970s, by rocket fire as well as by raiding parties (*44*).

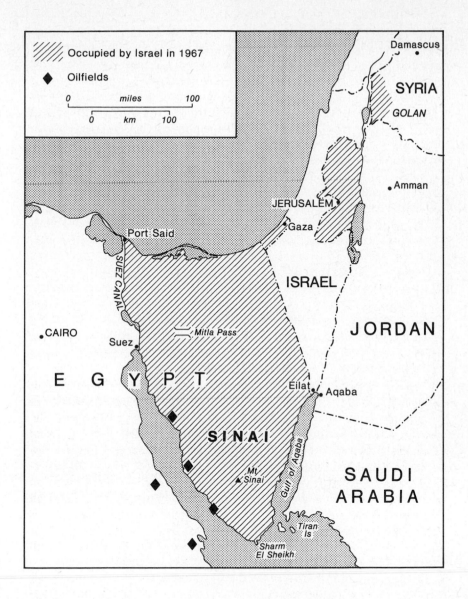

43 Israel and Arabs II

In October 1973 Egypt and Syria launched simultaneous attacks on Israel. The Syrians were quickly driven back, and the Israelis advanced to within 25 miles of Damascus. The Egyptians crossed the Suez Canal and began to move eastwards, but within two weeks an Israeli force had crossed the canal near Ismailia, turned south and encircled the two of Suez, cutting off an Egyptian army east of the southern end of the canal. This 'Yom Kippur War' (so called because Israel was performing the Yom Kippur rites when attacked) greatly heightened international tension. During the fighting America sent arms to Israel, the USSR sent arms to Egypt and Syria, and there were fears of a direct US–Soviet confrontation. Arab governments cut oil supplies to western countries, setting off the first wave of steep oil price rises that severely affected the world economy (3).

The UN obtained cease-fires, sent a second UNEF to Sinai and, early in 1974, provided a 'disengagement observer force' (UNDOF) to man a buffer zone between the Syrian and Israeli armies. A series of Israeli withdrawals in 1974–5 released the trapped Egyptian army and allowed Egypt to occupy the east bank of the canal (which was reopened in 1975), with UNEF 2 manning a buffer zone in Sinai. The United States then undertook a sustained effort to avert a further conflict, and an early warning system manned by American civilians was installed in Sinai to support the UN force's buffer role. Egypt's relations with the USSR, long its main arms supplier, deteriorated; increasingly Egypt sought American help. In 1977 President Anwar Sadat made a dramatic visit to Israel and started a series of talks.

In 1978 the Egyptian and Israeli leaders met as President Carter's guests at Camp David, his rural retreat north-west of Washington DC. In 1979 they signed a peace treaty based on the Camp David agreements. Israel began a new series of withdrawals, and the last of its forces left Sinai in 1982.

Other Arab governments, resenting the peace treaty, broke off relations with Egypt. (Most of them had resumed relations by 1987). The USSR blocked the renewal of UNEF's mandate, but the Americans were able to muster a replacement for it – the 'multinational force and observers' (MFO) installed in 1982 in a buffer zone running along the Egypt–Israel frontier and south to Sharm el Sheikh.

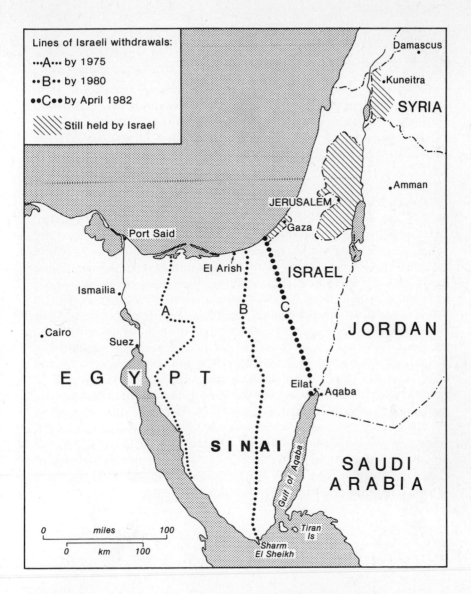

The peace treaty survived several subsequent crises, but there remained the problem of the West Bank and Gaza. The treaty had provided for negotiations with the aim of giving the 'occupied territories' autonomy, but the negotiations became deadlocked, while Israel went on creating Jewish settlements in the West Bank. Only 3,000 Jews lived there in 1975; 45,000 by

1985; 75,000 by 1987; nearly 100,000 by 1990 (and in East Jerusalem, solidly Arab in 1967, there were by 1990 about 150,000 Arabs and 150,000 Jews). Jewish settlement in the West Bank (and in a few places in the Gaza strip) had continued to grow in spite of the *intifada* (uprising) initiated in 1987 – an Arab campaign of stone-throwing, sniping, acts of arson, demonstrations and strikes which by 1990 had led to 1,000 deaths, mostly of Arabs. Of the 195,000 Soviet Jews who migrated to Israel in 1989–90 very few went to the West Bank, but the PLO denounced the USSR for letting them leave.

In 1990 there were about 3.9 million Jews in Israel; 1.7 million Arabs in the West Bank and Gaza, and 800,000 within Israel's pre-1967 boundaries; and, of the dispersed Palestinian Arabs, about 2.4 million in Jordan, Lebanon and Syria, 700,000 in the oil-producing Arab Gulf states (*40*) and 600,000 elsewhere. The PLO leaders, evicted from Beirut by the Israelis in 1982 and from north Lebanon by the Syrians in 1983 (*44*), had set up their headquarters in Tunisia, where in 1988 they proclaimed the independence of Palestine (without specifying its frontiers; many governments, mostly in the third world, recognized them as, in effect, a government in exile. Their statements about renouncing violence and living-in peace with Israel remained ambiguous – yet went too far to suit some of the hard-line terrorist groups backed by Iran, Libya, Iraq and, at times, Syria. But in early 1990, with Egypt readmitted to the Arab League in spite of its peaceful relations with Israel, and the PLO at last in direct contact with the United States (partly through Egypt's good offices), signs of progress towards a settlement seemed to emerge. By the end of the year, however, Iraq's aggression against Kuwait had split the Arab ranks again, alarmed the Israelis, set new problems for the PLO, left many thousands of the exiled Palestinians without jobs, put severe strain on Jordan and made the whole Middle East atmosphere unpropitious (*45*).

44 Lebanon

Being half Muslim, half Christian, Lebanon was given a special status under Turkish rule; under the French mandate (*42*) it was separated from Syria (whose rulers tend to regard the separation as temporary). The constitutional 'checks and balances' that were devised gave the Christians advantages that the Muslims came to resent; the Christians came to fear submergence in the surrounding Muslim world; and, among the Muslims, the Shias resented the Sunni's privileged position (*28*). Moreover, after 1970 the Palestine Liberation Organization (PLO) concentrated its forces in Lebanon (*42*), and its attacks on Israel brought reprisals. Under all these strains Lebanon eventually cracked. What had been almost the only liberal society in the Arab world went down into chaotic bloodshed.

In the confused civil war that broke out in 1975 the main conflicts were between the Palestinians, with some leftist, largely Shia, Lebanese allies, and the Maronites – the biggest Christian sect, named from the fifth-century St Maro. A sort of partition took shape, the Christians holding a zone running north from the capital, Beirut (which became a battlefield), while the PLO and its allies dominated the south and also held areas near the northern frontier. In 1976 Syria sent in troops; its intervention temporarily halted the fighting and was thus welcomed, but some Lebanese became suspicious as the Syrian troops' presence came to look more permanent.

In 1978 Israel, seeking to stop PLO raiding and rocket fire across its frontier, occupied Lebanon south of the river Litani. A UN force was sent to restore Lebanese authority in the south, but when the Israelis withdrew, after only three months, they handed over a 'security zone' along the border to a local militia which had been holding a Christian enclave around Marjayoun. Both this Israel-backed militia and the PLO harassed the UN force, which was deployed in two areas but could not even create a continuous buffer zone. In contrast, UNDOF (*43*), the UN force in Syria's Golan region, found both Syrians and Israelis accepting its control of its buffer zone.

In 1981, when the Syrians shelled Christian-held East Beirut and besieged Zahle, a Christian-held town in the Bekaa valley, fears of a new war increased. In 1982 it came. This time the Israelis advanced to Beirut, sidestepping the UN force, and cleared the PLO out of south Lebanon.

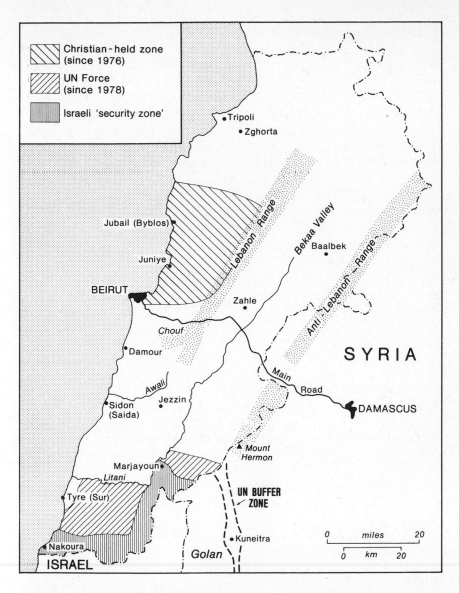

After a two-month siege of West Beirut the 11,000 PLO guerrillas who had
been trapped there were evacuated to other Arab states, and the PLO set
up new headquarters in Tunisia (*43*) – on which Israeli aircraft made a
reprisal attack in 1985. Israeli and Syrian troops faced each other along a
line running north-west from Mount Hermon; the Chouf hills, south-east

133

of Beirut, became the main stronghold of the Druzes, a community that broke away from Islam 900 years ago. A French–Italian–US peacekeeping force, with a small British contingent, was sent to Beirut.

In 1983 Syria forced the PLO out of north Lebanon; the Israelis pulled back to the river Awali; confused fighting, mostly in Beirut, was resumed – and went on, year after year – between the Lebanese factions' militias (Shia, Druze, Maronite, others) and, sometimes, resurfacing Palestinian guerrillas. 'Suicide bombers' killed 300 US and French soldiers of the four-power force, which was withdrawn in 1984. The Israelis completed

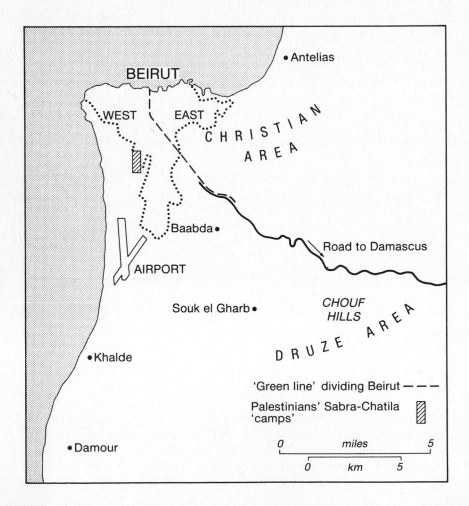

their withdrawal in 1985, and the Shia militia took over most of south Lebanon. Hardly any Europeans remained in West Beirut after a series of murders and hostage-takings, mostly by Hezbollah or other Iran-backed Shia gangs (47).

Lebanon's official army had been brushed aside by all parties during these turbulent years, but in 1988 its Christian commander, General Michel Aoun, launched a campaign to free Lebanon from Syrian domination. Nine-tenths of Beirut's 1.5 million inhabitants fled when, for several months in 1989, Aoun's shelling of West Beirut and the Syrians' shelling of East Beirut gave the city its worst battering yet; Syria blockaded the Christian areas by land and sea, and Beirut's seaport and airport were closed. Although most Christians supported Aoun, the main Maronite militia opposed and fought him. In 1990 Syria's army and air force finally defeated him; its hold on Lebanon became tighter than ever. In the south, around Sidon, rival Shia militias, one Iran-backed, one Syria-backed, fought each other, sometimes tangling with the PLO too. (The PLO leaders had sided with Iraq against Syria.) The Druze militia still held the Chouf; the Maronites held part of the former Christian zone north of Beirut; Syria effectively controlled all other areas, except the Israeli 'security zone' in the far south – which sometimes seemed to stretch as far as Jezzin. One more attempt was made to put together a generally acceptable Lebanese government: but all such attempts had failed for the past 15 years.

45 Iraq and Arabia

In 1990 Iraq's invasion and occupation of Kuwait, the world-wide reactions, and the mustering of a large American-led international force in Saudi Arabia near the Kuwait frontier, focused attention on the Arabian peninsula and on the Arab lands north of it.

The 1914–18 war had ended Turkey's domination of the region. Iraq came under British rule until 1932, and Syria under French rule until 1946 (42). In 1955 Iraq joined Britain, Iran, Pakistan and Turkey in the US-backed Baghdad Pact, but withdrew when its pro-western government was overthrown in 1958 – after which Iraq was ruled by military regimes. (The Baghdad Pact was reshaped as the Central Treaty Organization, often called CENTO, which was ended in 1979.) Some of Iraq's oilfields (40) are among its northern mountains, whose Kurdish inhabitants have often rebelled and been brutally subdued (48). Of Iraq's 17 million people, 4 million are Kurds; two-thirds of the Arabs are Shia Muslims, but the rulers are Sunnis (28).

Syria, after spending 1958–61 linked with Egypt in the short-lived United Arab Republic (29), was also ruled by a series of military regimes, sometimes with great brutality; in 1982, after a rising at Hama (42), the army killed 20,000 people there. Since 1976 the Syrian army has occupied part of Lebanon (44). Its old rivalry with Iraq has turned to enmity; during the Iran–Iraq war, Syria even sided with non-Arab Iran (48).

The Saudi Arabian kingdom had taken its present shape by 1934. From a base among the Wahabi (puritan) Arabs of the Nejd, the Saud family had extended its power over the Hasa, Hejas and Asir regions. From 1939 on, oilfields in Hasa turned a desert country into the world's biggest oil exporter (3, 40). The Saudis often subsidized other Arab states – notably Egypt, Syria and Iraq – and they also financed the PLO (42); after the 1970s' oil price rises, Saudi decisions on output, and on the disposition of funds, affected the world economy. Saudi Arabia remained a very conservative country – the guardian of Islam's holiest place, Mecca (28, 29). Pilgrimages to Mecca were disrupted in the 1980s by large Iranian contingents who staged demonstrations there; after violent clashes, the Saudis limited the Iranians' numbers. Iran launched an anti-Saudi propaganda campaign (47).

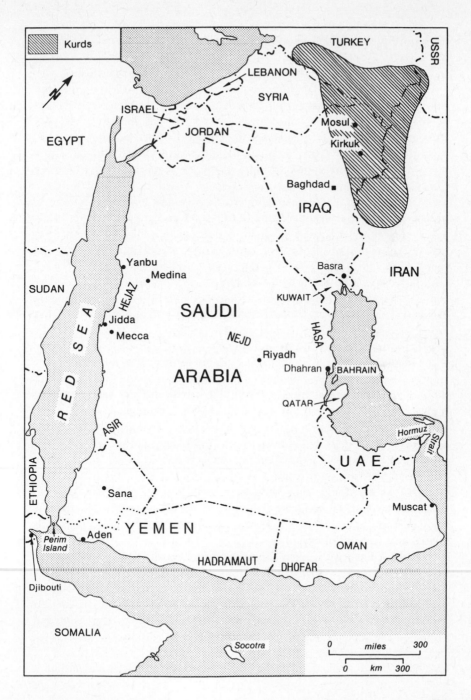

Kurds

TURKEY

USSR

LEBANON

SYRIA

ISRAEL

JORDAN

Mosul

Kirkuk

EGYPT

Baghdad ▪

IRAQ

SUDAN

Yanbu

Medina

Basra

IRAN

KUWAIT

RED SEA

HEJAZ

SAUDI

NEJD

HASA

Jidda

Mecca

Riyadh

Dhahran

BAHRAIN

ARABIA

QATAR

ASIR

Hormuz

Strait

U.A.E.

ETHIOPIA

Sana

Muscat

Perim
Island

Aden

Y E M E N

OMAN

Djibouti

HADRAMAUT

DHOFAR

SOMALIA

Socotra

0   miles   300

0   km   300

South Arabia's two Yemeni states agreed to merge in 1990, after years of toing and froing. Britain's former Aden protectorate had become independent South Yemen in 1967. The far-left groups that took it over gave the USSR naval facilities in the port of Aden and at Perim and Socotra islands (*41*). These groups were incompetent and feud-ridden, and in 1986 they clashed in open battle in Aden; all foreigners (mostly Russians) were hastily evacuated to Djibouti. The ending of Soviet subsidies left South Yemen virtually bankrupt and forced it to agree to a merger with the more populous, more fertile, and less poor (since it struck oil) 'North' Yemen – officially, just Yemen – which, although formerly torn by civil wars, had a more moderate regime and longer experience of independence. Apart from the small Gulf states (*46*), the peninsula's only other country was Oman, a sultanate which became fully independent in 1970 after a period of British protection. Oman, the small Gulf states, and Saudi Arabia formed the Gulf Co-operation Council (GCC) in 1981 (*46*).

When Iraq's 1980–8 war with Iran ended (*48*), Iraq was left with a huge army, a battered economy and a frustrated, ambitious ruler, Saddam Hussein Takriti. It was detected trying to acquire components for long-range 'super-guns' and for nuclear weapon production; it was known to be producing missiles at Karbala and poison gas at Samarra (*48*). Its fellow Arab neighbours feared that, having failed against Iran, it would seek weaker victims. Iraq was soon pressing Kuwait to hand over a border oilfield and the uninhabited Bubiyan island. In August 1990 it seized Kuwait – which resisted, but was soon overrun. Saddam said he would withdraw his troops as soon as a new Kuwaiti government was formed; a few days later, he declared Kuwait to be a permanent part of Iraq.

About half Kuwait's population fled or were forced to go; thousands of immigrant workers, mostly from southern Asia, Egypt and Jordan, fled from both Kuwait and Iraq. Altogether, a million people, many of them destitute, got out, the majority crossing the desert to Jordan. Meanwhile Saddam kept thousands of Europeans, Americans and Russians in Iraq as virtual hostages until December.

The UN Security Council, in resolutions mostly backed by all five permanent members (*8*), ordered Iraq to withdraw, imposed a trade embargo and other 'sanctions', and authorized the use of 'all necessary means' to make Iraq withdraw if it had not done so by mid-January 1991. At an Arab League 'summit' (*29*) a majority condemned Iraq's aggression and approved the sending of troops to Saudi Arabia in response to appeals for help.

The embargo prevented Iraq from exporting its oil (or the Kuwaiti oil it

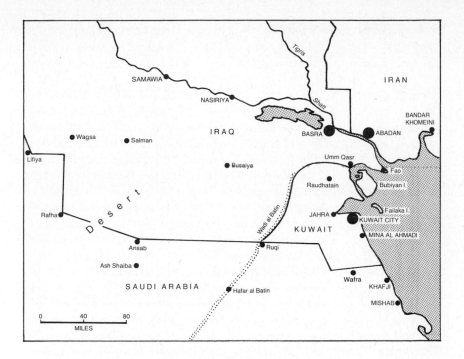

had seized). When the Turks and the Saudis shut off the pipelines carrying Iraqi oil across their territories (40) the Saudis were at once in danger of retaliatory attack. (Turkey, a well-armed member of NATO, was much less at risk.) US troops were rushed to Saudi Arabia, followed by many others. By the end of 1990 ground and air force units had arrived from the US, Britain, France, Canada; seven Arab states: Bahrain, Egypt, Morocco, Oman, Qatar, Syria, the UAE; and four other Muslim countries: Bangladesh, Niger, Pakistan, Senegal. Warships had been sent by several of these and also by Argentina, Australia, Belgium, Denmark, Greece, Holland, Italy, Norway, Spain and the USSR.

It had been the first case of one Arab League member engulfing another, and the first case of one UN member state engulfing another with the declared intention of permanent annexation. Saddam appealed for Arab and Muslim support, and for general anti-American support, and tried to pose as the Palestinians' champion, saying that if Iraq was attacked he would strike at Israel. But the wide line-up against him reflected fears that, if such blatant aggression succeeded, others would be encouraged.

46 Gulf states

World politics sometimes muddles geographical terms. The Arabian peninsula (*45*) was, for centuries, ringed by the Red Sea or Arabian Gulf, the Arabian Sea (part of the Indian Ocean), and the Persian Gulf (between Arabia and Iran, or Persia). Some Arabs wanted the Persian Gulf to be called the Arabian Gulf; that would have led to more confusion, so it is now usually just called the Gulf – which is bad enough, as, in oilmen's jargon, 'Gulf' may also refer to the Gulf of Mexico.

Saudi Arabia has sometimes been called a Gulf state (although its Red Sea coast is much longer); so has Oman (which is outside the Gulf, except for a small enclave at the Hormuz strait). But, strictly, the Gulf states are four small ones: Kuwait, Bahrain, Qatar and the United Arab Emirates (UAE). All were formerly under British protection by treaty (Kuwait, for example, by a treaty of 1899). Kuwait became fully independent in 1961, Bahrain, Qatar and the UAE in 1971 (*41*). The UAE had been formed by Abu Dhabi, Dubai, Sharjah, Ajman, Umm al Qaiwain, Ras al Khaimah and Fujairah – once known as the Trucial States; their pacts with Britain had included the 1853 Perpetual Maritime Truce.

Iran, which had long maintained a claim to Bahrain, renounced it in 1970. Iraq abandoned a claim to Kuwait in 1963 – after threatening to annex the country in 1961. A small British force, sent to protect Kuwait against that 1961 threat, had soon been replaced by a joint Arab League force; the other Arab states never accepted Iraq's claim, as Kuwait had never been part of an independent Iraq. (Both had once been within the old Turkish empire, but so had almost all the Arab states.)

In 1981 the small Gulf states joined Saudi Arabia and Oman in forming the Gulf Co-operation Council. All six GCC members had oilfields and were enriched by the 1970s oil price rises (*3*). The oil boom brought them many thousands of immigrant workers from southern Asia; Palestinian Arabs were also numerous in the oilfield regions (*43*). Along the Arab side of the Gulf there are also some small Iranian communities, and larger communities of Shia Arabs (*28*); Iran's influence among these Shias has at times troubled the GCC states' Sunni rulers.

Where the Saudi–Kuwait frontier nears the sea a small area called the Neutral Zone was jointly controlled by the two states from 1922 to 1966;

they then partitioned it, but went on sharing, and haggling over, its large oil revenues. During the Iran–Iraq war one of the ways they subsidized Iraq was by giving it the profits from sales of the zone's oil. Iraq showed a strange kind of gratitude when, in 1990, it seized Kuwait – with half the zone (45).

47 Iran

In Iran (Persia) not much more than half the 52 million people are Farsi-speaking Persians. More than a quarter are Azerbaijani (or Azeri) Turks. Near the western frontiers there are Kurdish and Arab minorities, near the eastern ones Turkmens and Baluchs (*45, 48, 49*).

During the 1939–45 war British and Soviet forces occupied Iran, and the western allies sent vital supplies to the USSR across it. In 1945 the USSR, angry because the Iranians would not grant it oilfield concessions, held on to the north-western regions and set up puppet Azerbaijani and Kurdish governments there. Western pressure made the Soviet forces leave in 1946, but Iran's fear of the USSR had been heightened. Although post-war Iran asserted itself against western economic power, expropriating the British oil company in 1951 (*40*), it joined the western-backed Baghdad Pact in 1955 (*45*). Later it strengthened its armed forces with aid and encouragement from the United States, which hoped that Iran would be a barrier against Soviet encroachment into the Middle East.

In the 1970s the regime headed by the Shah met mounting internal opposition. The Shah's enthusiasm for education and social reform angered Muslim mullahs; his reliance on American help angered leftists. Religious and revolutionary forces, both able to foment mob violence, joined hands. By the end of 1978 Iran was in turmoil, and its oil exports had been halted, setting off the second big wave of world-wide oil price rises (*3*). In 1979 the Shah was forced into exile and power passed into the hands of fanatical Islamic fundamentalists (*28*). Religious persecution and arbitrary executions on a massive scale soon made the new regime appear far more oppressive than the old one.

Iran denounced the 1979 Soviet invasion of Afghanistan, which sent millions of Afghan refugees fleeing into both Iran and Pakistan (*49*). But Iran's new rulers were more intent on hounding the Americans. In November 1979 the US embassy in Teheran was seized and its staff were held as hostages. During 1980 the Americans tried to rescue them, but the hostages were not released until January 1981. Iran's violation of the rules of diplomacy was widely condemned, and its self-imposed isolation encouraged Iraq to invade it (*48*).

The Iranian pseudo-theocracy made ruthless use of religious fanaticism

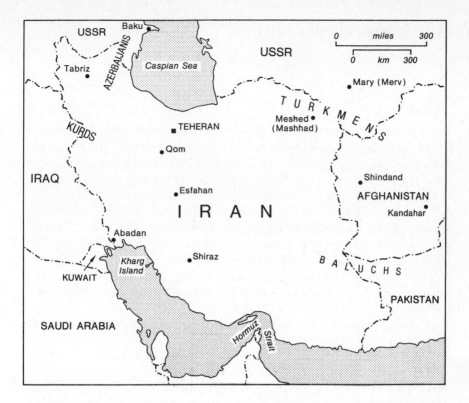

far beyond its borders. It failed to turn the Shias of Iraq against the Iraqi regime by demanding that they should side with Iran, the Shias' chief stronghold in the Muslim world (*28*). But in other Arab states the call for Shia loyalty often prevailed over Arab suspicions of Iran. Iran paid, armed and at least partly directed some guerrilla groups which, while helping to wreck Lebanon by sectarian fighting, specialized in exploiting western civilians as hostages. Iran thundered against the 'satanic' Americans and Israelis even (the US 'Irangate' hearings in 1987 revealed) while it was buying Israeli arms from the Americans. In 1989 it issued a call for the murder of an author whose offence was to have published a 'blasphemous' book in Britain (*28*).

48 Iran—Iraq war

The 1980–8 war between Iran and Iraq followed a period of disputes between them, particularly over control of the Shatt al Arab, the waterway through which the Euphrates and Tigris flow into the Gulf, and on which stand Basra, Iraq's port, and Iran's port of Khorramshahr and Abadan oil refineries. Iraq wooed the Arab inhabitants of Iran's Khuzestan province. Iran urged Iraq's Shia Muslims to throw off their Sunni rulers (*28*). After minor frontier clashes, Iraq invaded Iran in the belief that it could show little resistance, being still in turmoil after the ousting of the Shah (*47*). This belief proved mistaken. But Iran did have one advantage: Iran's self-inflicted isolation, partly the result of its flouting of international law and custom by holding diplomats as hostages. Iran, when attacked, found few sympathizers.

The Iraqi invaders captured only one large city, Khorramshahr. By 1982 they had been pushed back to the frontier in most sectors, and Iraq was already suing for peace; but Iran was now vowing that it would bring Iraq to its knees. From the start the war had blocked all Iraq's trade through Basra and its oil shipments through the Gulf. Iraq exported its oil through pipelines running across Turkey to the Mediterranean, and across Saudi Arabia to the Red Sea (*40*), but an older pipeline across Syria was denied to it, the Syrians having sided with Iran against their fellow Arab Iraqis. For its imports Iraq depended on costly road transport from Kuwait, or Jordan, or Turkey. To pay for his war, its ruler, Saddam Hussein Takriti, borrowed huge sums from Kuwait and Saudi Arabia, which also made generous gifts to their fellow Arab; but, even with this help, Iraq's economy was almost wrecked by the war Saddam had plunged it into.

Iran's fanatical rulers proclaimed a holy war (*28, 47*) and used 'human sea' tactics, sending wave after wave of men, and often children, to be mown down. (Iraq's war dead exceeded 250,000, but Iranian losses were far heavier.) The Iranian forces eventually got close enough to Basra to shell the city. In 1986 they crossed the Shatt near its mouth and got a toehold on Iraqi territory at Fao, which they held until 1988.

What was then often called 'the Gulf war' did not involve much fighting

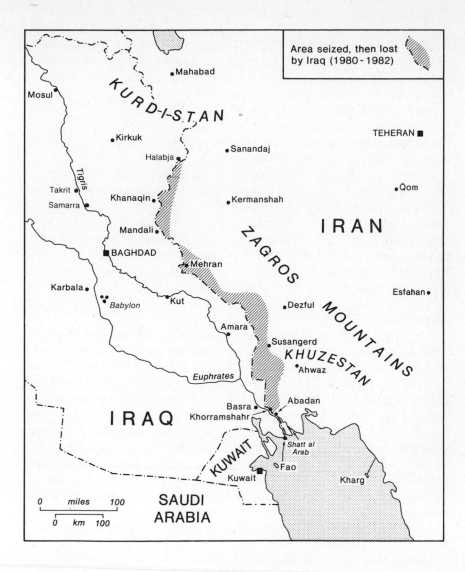

Area seized, then lost by Iraq (1980-1982)

Mahabad

Mosul

KURD-I-STAN

TEHERAN ■

Kirkuk

Sanandaj

Halabja

Qom

Tigris

Takrit
Samarra

Khanaqin

Kermanshah

IRAN

Mandali

ZAGROS

■ BAGHDAD

Mehran

Karbala

Babylon

Kut

Dezful

Esfahan

MOUNTAINS

Amara

Susangerd

KHUZESTAN

Euphrates

Ahwaz

IRAQ

Basra
Khorramshahr

Abadan

Shatt al
Arab

KUWAIT

Fao

Kharg

Kuwait

0   miles   100

0   km   100

SAUDI
ARABIA

145

in the Gulf itself until 1984, when Iraq started air attacks on Kharg, the main Iranian oil terminal. Iran began to retaliate against ships using Kuwaiti and Saudi ports, refusing to regard them as neutral. The 'tanker war' developed steadily: in 1984 51 ships were attacked; by 1987 the year's count was 178. Kuwait's oil exports (which all went by sea) were particularly imperilled by Iranian missiles, mines and fast gunboats, and in 1987 the United States took over some Kuwaiti tankers, 'reflagging' them, and escorting them through the Gulf in convoy.

By then US, British, French and other minesweepers had been sent to the Gulf, and the international array of 75 warships there included Soviet ones, sent to protect Soviet tankers chartered by Kuwait. Iran had threatened to close the Gulf to all shipping – by using Chinese missiles which it deployed near the Strait of Hormuz (47) – but the maritime powers' angry reaction deterred it. Because it was Iran that deliberately attacked neutral ships, and because Iraq had long been seeking peace, Iran was as unpopular as ever, and UN pressure for a cease-fire, with the major powers all more or less behind it, was directed mainly at Iran. In 1988 the UN got a cease-fire, finally constraining a sullen Iran.

Iraq promptly claimed a great victory. In reality Saddam had attained none of his objectives. The Shatt remained blocked; control of it remained in dispute; over 100,000 prisoners of war remained behind barbed wire. Peace talks were stalled. But in August 1990, when Saddam found he had made yet another costly mistake by underestimating the international reaction to his seizure of Kuwait (45), he saw that he must conciliate Iran so that he could transfer troops from the Iranian frontier to his Kuwaiti front. He asked Iran to agree to an exchange of prisoners of war, and withdrew his troops from the pockets of Iranian territory they still held. And he agreed that control of the Shatt al Arab should be shared, with a midstream dividing line, thus abandoning his primary war aim of obtaining full Iraqi control of the waterway. The 'victory' that Saddam claimed he had won for Iraq meant in practice that, after eight ruinous years of war, nothing had been gained.

During their war Iraq and Iran had both faced rebellions, in the northern sectors of the war zone, by their Kurdish communities. The Kurds, a Muslim people whose language is distantly related to Persian, inhabit a large mountainous area (45) in Iran, Iraq, Syria, Turkey and the Soviet borderlands. There are about 5 million in Iran, 4 million in Iraq (forming a quarter of the population), 10 million in Turkey and a million in Syria and the USSR. In 1988 Iraqi troops, using poison gas, killed over 4,000 civilian Kurds at Halabja in one day; then, using more gas, they destroyed 3,000 Kurdish villages and drove 100,000 Kurds into refugee camps in Turkey. By mid-1989 about 500,000 Kurds had been transported to camps in Iraq's desert areas.

49 Afghanistan

The Soviet invasion of Afghanistan in 1979 had many fateful consequences. Almost all the third-world states united in condemning it; it widened the rift between the USSR and China; and discontent inside the USSR grew as it became clear that Afghan resistance was continuing and Soviet casualties were steadily mounting. But not until 1989 was the USSR able to withdraw the occupying army, writing off its ten-year war as a failure. That war had taken well over a million lives – mostly Afghan civilians' – and nearly 2.5 million Afghans had fled into Iran, over 3 million into Pakistan, forming the world's largest refugee group.

Afghanistan has no ethnic or linguistic unity. In a pre-1979 population of about 17 million the largest groups were the 8 million Pathans (or Pushtuns), the 4 million Tajiks, about 1.5 million Uzbeks and a million Hazaras. The Tajiks and Uzbeks have kindred across the frontier to the north, in regions that Russia conquered in the nineteenth century (53); the Pathans have kindred in Pakistan, the Baluchs in Pakistan and Iran, the Turkmens in Iran and the USSR. Historically, Afghanistan's frontiers simply marked out the area which Pathan rulers based in Kabul had been able to hold, in the face of local rebelliousness and the imperial ambitions of Iran (Persia), Russia and the British in India.

After 1947 (50) the Kabul government pressed for Pakistan's North West Frontier Province to be made a sovereign state, 'Pushtunistan'. Afghanistan's propaganda campaign envenomed its relations with Pakistan, and disrupted its traditional trade routes to and through that country. Soviet influence in Kabul correspondingly increased. The Russians built roads and airfields whose military value later became clear; and they acquired the right to exploit the big gasfield near Shibarghan, from which a pipeline was built to the Soviet frontier. Military coups in 1973 and 1978 put a fairly pliant pro-Soviet regime in power in Kabul, but the Afghans grew more and more restive, and the Soviet officers who were attached to the Afghan army found that they could not rely on it.

In December 1979 Soviet troops were rushed to Kabul and other key points. Afghanistan's president was killed and a more docile successor installed, but the Afghans did not accept the occupation as tamely as the Soviet leadership had expected. A long war began, and the disintegration

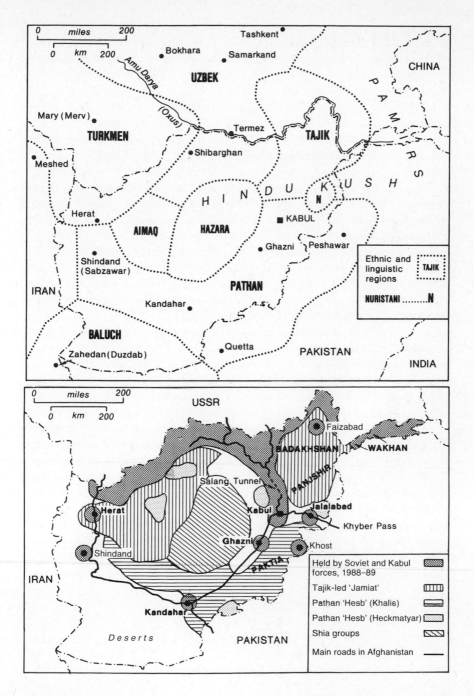

of the Kabul regime's army (many conscripts went over to join the guerrillas) left the Soviet forces to do more fighting than they had bargained for. Many villages were destroyed, and large areas devastated, by the greatly superior firepower of the Soviet forces (hence the huge exodus of refugees), but the *mujaheddin* (resistance fighters) extended their activity right across the country, even into the Uzbek regions along the Soviet border. Arms, money and other aid reached the guerrillas not only from Pakistan and Iran but from such varied sources as China, Saudi Arabia and the USA.

By 1988 the resistance controlled three-quarters of Afghanistan, had encircled Herat, Kandahar and other Soviet-held towns so that they had to be supplied by air, and was able to bombard Kabul itself. The USSR and its Kabul clients agreed that all the Soviet forces should be withdrawn by February 1989, their departure to be supervised by UN observers. The Soviet withdrawal reduced the bloodshed but did not end it. Some of the resistance groups were already fighting each other; some made informal truce agreements with the Kabul regime, while others stepped up their attacks on its garrison towns (notably Jalalabad) and its lines of communication (notably the Salang pass and tunnel linking Kabul with the Soviet frontier). The USSR was still spending huge sums to prop up the regime, and flying many planeloads of food into Kabul every day when the airport was not closed by guerrilla action, but by the end of 1990 the USSR had urged its Kabul clients to offer peace terms, even to the Afghan monarchists, and they had duly done so.

At least for a time it seemed that Afghanistan might revert to a familiar old pattern, its various regions controlled by local masters who might make deals with a nominal government in Kabul but would not take orders from it. But, while the Kabul regime was hastily abandoning Marxism, the resistance groups were still divided not only along tribal lines but also by doctrine – orthodox Sunni Muslims opposing dissident Shias backed by Iran (*28*); Islamic fundamentalists opposing monarchists and other 'moderates'. With all this, and some keen personal rivalries among the resistance leaders, there were fears that, even if Afghanistan was going to settle for a fragmented future, there would first be a good deal more fighting.

50 India and Pakistan I

Britain's Indian empire was the most spectacular feature of the age of colonization in Asia and Africa, and it was the British withdrawal from India that set off the great wave of 'decolonization' (9, 27). Until the 1930s, proposals for India's advance to independence were based on the hope that the unity brought to the 'sub-continent' by the British could be preserved. But the Muslims (a quarter of undivided India's population of about 45 million) began to demand a separate state, to be called Pakistan, and it seemed that, to avert an all-out Hindu–Muslim war, there must be a partition. Even so, before and after the two nations became independent in 1947, there was much bloodshed in Punjab and Bengal, the two provinces that had to be divided, as half of their inhabitants were Muslims. Half a million people were killed; 8 million Muslims fled from India into Pakistan and a similar number of Hindus and Sikhs fled in the opposite direction. However, 10 million Hindus remained in Pakistan, and 40 million Muslims in India (where there are now 100 million Muslims, 12% of the population).

Pakistan emerged with two 'wings', separated by 1,000 miles of Indian territory, each with half of the population. Bengalis complained that the government – based at first in Karachi, later in Islamabad – always favoured the western wing, which comprised Sind, Baluchistan, the North West Frontier Province and the western part of Punjab (51).

Most of the princely states which had formerly accepted British paramountcy acceded to one or other of the two new nations. The Muslim ruler of Hyderabad (mainly Hindu-peopled) sought independence, but India took over his state in 1948. The Hindu ruler of Kashmir (mainly Muslim-peopled) vacillated; a Muslim revolt broke out, and Pathan tribesmen from Pakistan invaded Kashmir. Its ruler asked India for help, offering accession. India sent troops in, but the Muslims still held north-west Kashmir in 1949, when the UN secured a cease-fire and sent in military observers (8). The Kashmir problem caused several later crises, some of them involving China (51, 52).

Sri Lanka (until 1972 Ceylon), a separate British colony, became independent in 1948. Its relations with India were complicated by the problem of its Tamil minority (about a fifth of the population of 16

million). Some of their ancestors had come from India in the nineteenth century, but more than half of them represent a community that has been in the island for 1,000 years, mostly in the north and east. In the 1950s moves to impose more use of Sinhala, the language of the majority, led to a series of conflicts with the Tamils. Concessions were made on the language question, but violent clashes began again in the 1980s. In 1983 thousands of Tamils living in Colombo were driven from their homes. By 1986 Tamil 'Tiger' guerrillas controlled the Jaffna area and were trying to take over Trincomalee. The Tigers used bases in the Tamil Nadu province of India (51), but India refused to back them. In 1987, by agree-

ment with Sri Lanka's government, India sent 50,000 soldiers to the island's north and east regions, aiming to round up and disarm the guerrillas. But in 1990 the Indian troops withdrew, and fighting was soon resumed in the north between Tigers and government forces. To conciliate the Tamils, a fairly wide autonomy had been offered to the north and east regions; but, while the north was almost solidly Tamil, they were outnumbered in the east by the Sinhalese (mainly Buddhists) and the 'Moors' (Muslims who, although mostly Tamil-speakers, originated from various parts of India). The guerrillas wanted both north and east to be formed into an independent Tamil state, to be called Eelam.

During the period of British rule, France and Portugal held small coastal territories in India. The French ones were handed over to India in 1951 and 1954. Portugal would not agree to a transfer, but in 1961 India took over Goa, Diu and Daman, the last vestiges of European rule in the subcontinent.

51 India and Pakistan II

In 1965 moves to integrate Kashmir more fully into India heightened tension. After Pakistani infiltration across the 1949 cease-fire line (50), Indian troops launched attacks across the line; Pakistan counter-attacked; Indian forces invaded Pakistan itself, in the Punjab and Sind sectors. The UN obtained a cease-fire, and sent observers to watch over the two armies' withdrawal (8), which was completed in six months.

By 1971 Bengali demands for more self-government for East Pakistan had met with repressive action, a large part of Pakistan's army was fighting Bengali guerrillas, and several million Bengalis had fled into India. India's army invaded East Pakistan and defeated the Pakistani forces there. A new independent republic, Bangladesh, was proclaimed in what had been East Pakistan.

Bangladesh's independence was eventually acknowledged by Pakistan, but friction between the two continued over many issues, including exchanges of population. And, although Bangladesh owed its independence to India, there were disputes between these two: over control of the waters of the rivers Ganges and Brahmaputra, whose joint delta covers most of Bangladesh; and over illegal Bengali migration into Assam, which caused so much unrest there that by 1990 India was having to suppress separatist agitation.

Meanwhile India had laid out a new set of state boundaries. Its former princely states were absorbed, and the new states were based mainly on linguistic regions: Kerala, for speakers of Malayalam; Tamil Nadu, for Tamil; Andhra Pradesh, for Telugu; Karnataka (until 1973 Mysore) for Kanarese (Kannada); Gujarat, for Gujarati-speakers; Maharashtra, for Marathi; Orissa, for Oriya; West Bengal, for Bengali; Rajasthan, Uttar Pradesh, Madhya Pradesh and Bihar, for Hindi and its variants. In 1966 the part of Punjab left to India by partition was redivided: the mainly Hindi-speaking part became Haryana, the Himalayan foothills went to Himachal Pradesh, the residual Punjab being mainly Punjabi-speaking and predominantly (about 60%) Sikh.

In the north-east, Assam was diminished by the creation of new states for the peoples of the hill areas around the Brahmaputra valley: Nagaland, with its capital at Kohima, for the Nagas; Mizoram (formerly the Lushai

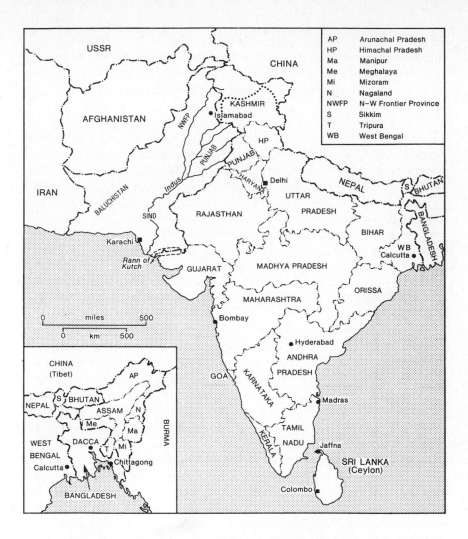

Hills); Meghalaya, for the Garo, Khasi and Jaintia hill peoples; Arunachal
Pradesh (formerly the North East Frontier Agency, NEFA). Manipur and
Tripura, former princely states, were given full statehood. Separatist guerrilla campaigns had ended in Nagaland in the 1970s and in Mizoram in the
mid-1980s; there had been more sporadic trouble in Manipur.

Vast and variegated India, the world's biggest democracy, has to
contend with hundreds of linguistic, religious and cultural divisions.
These do not all involve demands for independence: during the 1980s, for

155

instance, Ghurkas (immigrants from Nepal) around Darjeeling in northernmost West Bengal launched a 'national liberation' movement but, after three years and 200 killings, accepted local autonomy. The worst conflicts have involved religious divisions: between Muslims, Sikhs and Hindus; between 'higher' and 'lower' Hindu castes.

Sikh separatists' campaigns of terrorism in Punjab led in 1984 to military action against their stronghold in the Golden Temple of Amritsar (the Sikhs' holiest shrine), followed by mutinies by some Sikh soldiers; by the murder of India's prime minister, Mrs Indira Gandhi, by her own Sikh bodyguards; and by retaliatory killings of thousands of Sikhs in Delhi. In 1990 Sikh terrorism was still taking 500 lives a month in Punjab. By then Hindu–Muslim clashes were sorely afflicting other states. One cause was a new upsurge of secessionist agitation in Kashmir. Another was a campaign by Hindu fanatics to destroy mosques which, they complained, had been built at Hindu holy places – in particular at Ayodhya in Uttar Pradesh, where a mosque built in 1528 was attacked by huge crowds in 1990. Among Hindus there had been a violent reaction from higher castes when the government announced plans to reserve more official jobs for the disadvantaged lower castes.

Pakistan, although almost entirely Muslim since shedding its east wing in 1971, also suffered divisive strains: between the usually dominant Punjabis and the three other provinces; and, particularly in Karachi and other cities in Sind, between the old-established communities and such newcomers as Pathans (49) and *Mohajirs* ('refugees') – groups that had fled from India in 1947 or soon afterwards. The huge camps of refugees from Afghanistan posed another potentially acute problem, although these refugees were mainly Pathans, encamped in Pathan regions.

In a new attempt to improve relations between the countries of the southern Asia region, the South Asian Association for Regional Co-operation (SAARC) was created in 1985, at a meeting held in Dacca, by the prime minister of India, the presidents of Bangladesh, the Maldives (41), Pakistan and Sri Lanka, and the kings of Bhutan and Nepal (52). It was decided to establish a secretariat in Katmandu.

52 Himalayas

The Himalayan mountain range, formerly regarded as a clear natural dividing line, has become the scene of many disputes and clashes. Asia's strategic geography has changed. Previously India, so often invaded through the Afghan passes in the north-west, had never been seriously threatened from the north-east.

Tibet, although under China's formal suzerainty, was for centuries independent in practice, and ruled by successive Dalai Lamas who were also the religious leaders of a devoutly Buddhist people. In 1950 its small army could not prevent the occupation of Tibet by the communist forces which had won China's civil war (*54*). Large numbers of Chinese were settled in Tibet. Several revolts were suppressed. During one of them, in 1959, the Dalai Lama escaped to India.

Meanwhile China was publishing claims to Himalayan mountain areas long regarded as belonging to India, Nepal, Bhutan and Burma. There were border clashes near the Shipki Pass and elsewhere. The Chinese moved into the virtually empty Aksai Chin region in north-east Kashmir and built a military road across it from east to west. In 1959 there was a clash on the border north of Assam, where in 1914 the British who then ruled India and Burma had fixed (after negotiating with China and Tibet) the frontier called the McMahon Line. These border disputes worsened, and in 1962 the Chinese launched full-scale attacks in both sectors. In the north-east their forces advanced almost to the edge of the Assam plains. Two months later they pulled these forces back to the McMahon Line – but they did not renounce their claims in that sector, and in Kashmir they kept their hold on Aksai Chin.

China agreed on frontier lines with Nepal and Burma in 1960–1, accepting the Burmese part of the McMahon Line. In 1963 China agreed with Pakistan on a frontier line for part of Kashmir (*50*); Pakistan ceded part of the Karakoram range to China, despite Indian protests that it had no right to do so. In 1982 China and Pakistan opened a road across the range, linking Kashgar with Gilgit and Islamabad. Between 1982 and 1989 Indian and Pakistani forces repeatedly clashed around the Siachen glacier, in northernmost Ladakh. China had made gestures of support for Pakistan in the 1965 and 1971 India–Pakistan wars (*51*), continuing that support by

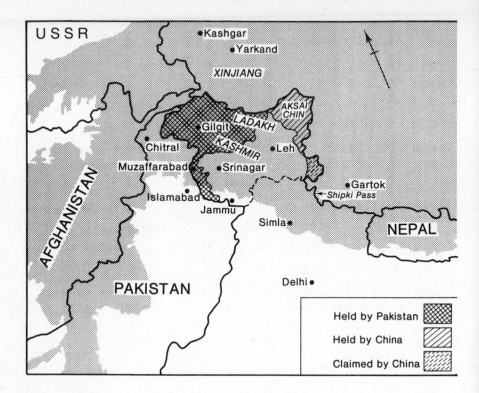

blocking Bangladesh's admission to membership of the United Nations for several years.

Nepal has a record of success in maintaining its independence. In its 1814–16 war against the British it so impressed them that agreements were made for them to recruit soldiers among the Ghurka tribes, Nepal's main ethnic element. For 130 years Gurkha regiments in British service showed their fighting quality in Europe and Africa as well as in Asia, and in 1947 Nepal agreed to let both Britain and newly independent India recruit Gurkha soldiers. Relations with India became frayed when Nepal's contacts with China increased (a new road now links Katmandu with the Tibet frontier). After Nepal's purchase of arms from China in 1988 India imposed a virtual blockade, closing the frontier crossing points when deadlock was reached in talks about a trade treaty. This rift continued into 1990.

Before 1947 Britain handled the external relations of Sikkim and Bhutan, and India succeeded it in this role. Sikkim became one of the

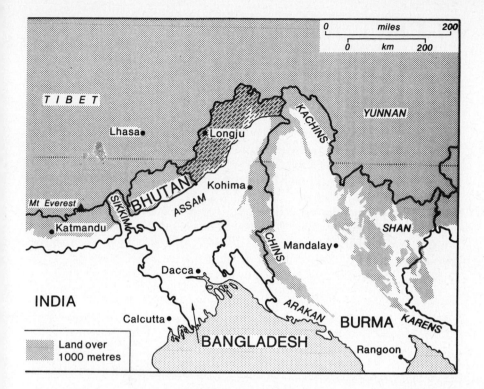

states of federal India in 1975. Bhutan chose to assert its identity by joining the United Nations in 1971. Later it became clear that Bhutan's identity was being changed by Nepalese immigration. By 1990 Nepalis made up 45% of its population of 1.3 million, and their agitation for political rights had led to outbreaks of violence.

Burma, to which the British gave independence in 1948 (only three years after driving the Japanese out of it), became in the 1960s a kind of new Tibet, deprived by its military rulers of almost all contact with the outside world. Once an important exporter of rice and oil, it was reduced to importing petrol in the 1980s, and even rice was scarce. The government had waged long wars against tribal rebels in the mountainous regions, particularly in the Karen areas.

53 China and USSR

In a long series of conquests, from 1580 to 1900, Russia and China took over the whole of northern Asia. Between them they subdued the Mongolians and all the Turkic-language peoples, from the Azerbaijanis of the Caucasus to the Yakuts of eastern Siberia, and including the Kazakhs, Tartars, Uzbeks and Uighurs.

Then the two empires clashed. In 1858 and 1860 the Russians annexed China's Pacific coast territory as far south as the border of Korea, near which they built their port and naval base of Vladivostok. In central Asia, Russia's annexations between 1845 and 1895 advanced its frontier from the Aral Sea to the present Soviet border (*41*), and the Russians asserted their

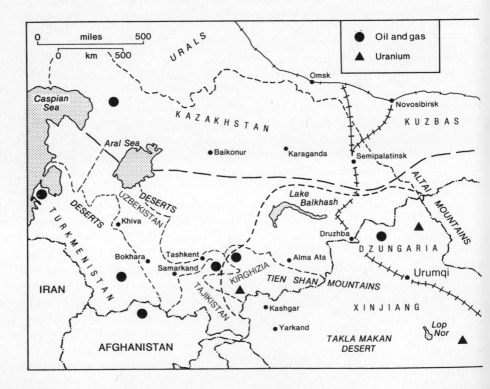

power in Xinjiang (Sinkiang, or Chinese Turkistan), Mongolia and Manchuria, regions nominally ruled by a then weak China. In 1898 Russia even acquired a naval base in China, at Port Arthur (now part of the city of Lüda); Japan seized this base in 1905, the USSR regained it in 1945, but in 1955 it was returned to China.

After Russia's 1917 revolutions the Turki peoples of central Asia tried to regain their independence, but by 1924 they had been reconquered (27). A million Kazakhs fled into China, and millions of Russians and other Europeans were settled in the USSR's central Asian regions. The Russians repelled China's attempts to regain control of Mongolia; after 1924 it was formally independent, in reality Soviet-controlled. The USSR annexed Tuvinia (Tannu-Tuva) in 1944.

After Japan's defeat in 1945 (57) Soviet troops occupied north-east China (Manchuria) for a time. In the 1950s, however, Xinjiang and Manchuria ceased to be Soviet spheres of influence; China took hold there, and settled millions of Chinese in Xinjiang (until then mainly peopled by

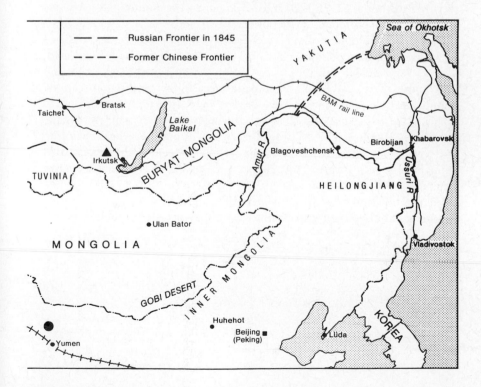

Turkic Uighurs and Kazakhs) and Inner Mongolia. When Sino-Soviet hostility developed in the 1960s (7) China began to complain that Russia had unfairly imposed parts of the frontier by nineteenth-century treaties. There were armed clashes, notably at Damansky island in the river Ussuri, north of Vladivostock. In 1974 the USSR, worried because its Trans-Siberian railway ran so close to the frontier, began to build the 2,000 mile Baikal–Amur (BAM) line farther to the north; it was declared complete in 1984 but in fact took five years longer. For both communist powers central Asia had become a site for nuclear test explosions – China's at Lop Nor lake, the USSR's near Semipalatinsk and elsewhere in Kazakhstan (10) – and a source of uranium.

In 1989 the USSR withdrew its troops from Afghanistan (49) and began to reduce its forces in Mongolia and along the Chinese frontier; it thus satisfied some of the demands made by China as conditions for a 'normalization' of relations. Tension was reduced, and work was resumed on a long abandoned project, the completion of a rail link between Urumqi and the Soviet frontier at Druzhba. Early in 1990 mass protests in Mongolia forced its rulers to announce reforms; at least on paper, the communist party was no longer to have a monopoly of power.

However, the news was less cheerful from Soviet central Asia – Kazakhstan (whose population is now 40% Russian) and the Turkmen, Uzbek, Tajik and Kirghiz republics. Old-style communist bosses were still in control there, although they made occasional gestures to Turkic national feeling and even to Islam. Troops were used to deal with riots in Uzbekistan, Tajikistan and Kirghizia during 1990's first half. Across the border, in Xinjiang, Chinese troops were flown to the Kashgar region to put down what was officially called a 'rebellion' among the Muslim inhabitants; the unrest spread to Urumqi, and apparently involved Kazakhs, Uighurs and Tajiks. China's rulers, having used the army to kill unarmed demonstrators and crush protest in Beijing itself in 1989, were evidently not going to loosen their grip on this westernmost corner of their empire.

54 China and other neighbours

After a century of weakness, exploited by Japan, Russia and several western states, China has again become the strongest east Asian power (*7, 10, 53*). In 1949 the communists' victory in China's civil war made it an ally of the USSR for a period during which it intervened in the Korean war (*58*) and supported the communist forces fighting in Indochina and the less successful communist guerrillas in Malaya (*60, 62*). China's new power aroused anxiety in South-East Asia, where 40 million 'overseas Chinese' live (*59, 63*). But these regional tensions were reduced by China's break with the USSR in the 1960s and its subsequent *rapprochement* with the USA (*7, 53*). Its communist rulers seemed in no great hurry to pursue their claims on Taiwan, Hong Kong and Macao (*55, 56*). In 1962 China fought a limited war against India (*52*), but from then until 1990 the only neighbour with which China came into large-scale violent conflict was communist-ruled Vietnam (*60*).

One of the clashes with Vietnam concerned a group of small islands, the Paracels (Xisha, or Hoang Sa), where Chinese forces repelled Vietnamese ones in 1982. In another group, the Spratlys (Mansha, or Truong Sa), Chinese warships sank several Vietnamese ships in a 1988 clash. Taiwan, Malaysia and the Philippines also have garrisons on some of the Spratlys, where their claims overlap – claims linked to hopes of finding offshore oilfields.

By the 1980s South Korea, Taiwan, Hong Kong and Singapore had become known as the four 'little dragons' because of the rapid economic progress made by these 'newly industrialised countries' (NICs), which had lifted them far above average third-world levels (*55, 56, 58, 62*). Three of these neighbours of China are themselves Chinese or mainly Chinese, while Korea's culture has been closely linked with China's for many centuries; hence the 'dragons' label.

On this map China's provinces and cities are given the spelling now officially approved in China. Some names (e.g. Yunnan, Shanghai) have not changed; for those that have, consult the index.

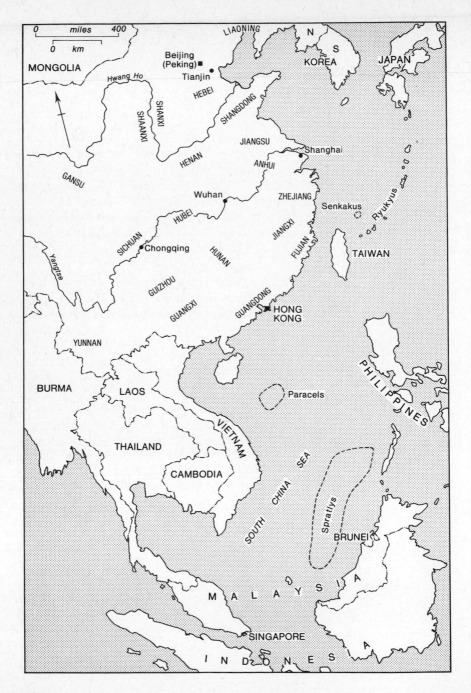

55 Taiwan

After the communists' victory in the 1946–9 Chinese civil war, Chiang Kai-shek's defeated Nationalist (Kuomintang) government took refuge in Taiwan (Formosa). Although ruled by Japan from 1895 to 1945, Taiwan had for centuries been a Chinese province, inhabited almost entirely by Chinese. Less than a fifth of its population of 20 million is of recent mainland origin; but these mainlanders kept all power in their hands for 30 years after 1949. They continued to insist that the rightful government of China was the one in Taipei. (It has been said that the only thing the two Chinas agree about is that there is only one China.) Until 1971 the Taipei government held China's seat at the UN (*8*), but during the 1970s the mainland government was recognized by the great majority of other states, including the USA (in 1990 only 25 were still recognizing the Taipei one).

In the 1950s American promises of protection for Taiwan had deterred the mainland regime from attacking it. Taiwan has kept garrisons on Quemoy, Matsu, Pratas and the Pescadores (Penghu) islands, and also on one of the Spratlys group (*54*); it claims the uninhabited Senkakus, where in 1990 it was in dispute with Japan. Although in the 1950s the mainland regime bombarded Quemoy, sometimes intensively, in later years it did not even challenge Taiwan's forces in the Spratlys. It expressed confidence that Taiwan would, in time, be reunited with China without war.

In the late 1980s opposition parties were legalized in Taiwan, martial law was ended, visits to the mainland were permitted, and, although trade with and investment in the mainland were still theoretically banned, in practice both boomed, the annual value of trade reaching $4,000 million. But these new links did not indicate that reunion was approaching. Its attraction was small for a Taiwan where income per head was 25 times the mainland figure. Meanwhile there were signs of an emerging Taiwanese identity. The island was still ruled by the Kuomintang party, but in 1990 it got its first Taiwan-born president, and in 1991 the last of the aged men who had sat in its legislature ever since 1949, nominally representing constituencies on the mainland, were due to retire.

56 Hong Kong

In the later nineteenth century China's coast was speckled with small European-ruled enclaves – British, French, German, Portuguese and Russian. After 1955, when Russia relinquished its base at Port Arthur (53), only Hong Kong and Macao remained.

The island of Hong Kong (on which the colony's capital, Victoria, stands) was ceded to Britain in 1842. The Kowloon area was ceded in 1860, and in 1898 the New Territories were acquired on a lease running to 1997. Hong Kong's population, which is 98% Chinese, has risen from 2.25 million in 1950 to about 5.75 million, largely because of huge influxes of refugees from the mainland since the communists' victory in the Chinese civil war (55). Although painfully crowded, Hong Kong has succeeded, like Singapore (62), in developing modernized manufacturing industry and raising income per head far above the Asian average.

However, it has only a few years ahead of it as Britain's last remaining populous colony. China, although willing to wait until 1997, when the New Territories lease expires, has made it clear that it will then insist on taking over the whole colony; and, after the transfer of the leased area, the remainder would be neither militarily defensible nor economically viable. Britain and China signed in 1984, and ratified in 1985, an agreement for the transfer of the whole of Hong Kong in 1997 to China, which undertook to allow it a degree of autonomy for 50 years thereafter.

In 1987 Portugal and China concluded a similar agreement, with a similar 50-year transitional period, for the transfer to China in 1999 of Macao – where the Portuguese had first settled in 1557. Since 1974 Macao (population 400,000, 97% Chinese) had been, officially, a Portuguese-administered piece of Chinese territory.

It was hoped that China would be more anxious to profit from the economic activity of Hong Kong and Macao than to destroy it. In 1979 it had established 'special economic zones' around Shenzhen and Zhuhai, chosen because they adjoined Hong Kong and Macao; foreign firms were given incentives to operate in these zones, taking advantage of low wages and producing mainly for export; by 1990 about 4,500 Hong Kong firms were active on the nearby mainland, providing work for 2 million people there. All this raised hopes; so did the general economic trend in China

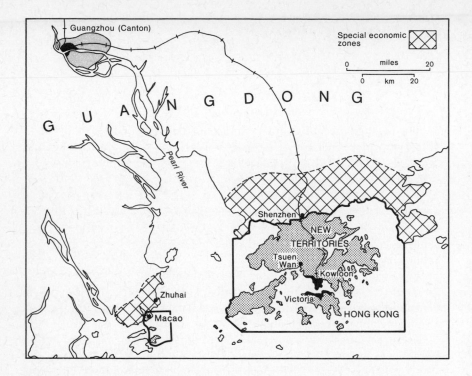

away from Marxist principles and towards market ones. But China opposed any political reform in Hong Kong, and in 1989 used its army to crush its own dissidents in Beijing (Peking). Each sign of political rigidity in China affected confidence in Hong Kong: its stock exchange index sagged; some rich people moved their money overseas and then followed it. Morale was not noticeably improved when the British government, in 1990, offered to provide 50,000 Hong Kong families with passports guaranteeing the right to live in Britain.

Until 1987 only about 4,000 'boat people' from Vietnam (59) were arriving in Hong Kong each year, but in 1988–9 about 54,000 arrived, the majority being classed as 'economic migrants', not political refugees. Few were accepted for resettlement in other countries; many Hong Kong people resented their presence, especially at a time when refugees from China were being turned away. For some, the only alternatives seemed to be a return to Vietnam or indefinite detention in a Hong Kong camp.

168

57 Japan's lost empire

Defeat in 1945 stripped Japan of an empire, acquired in 50 years of conquest, which at its peak embraced most of the Far East. After centuries of self-imposed isolation, Japan had embarked on a course of territorial expansion in 1895. By 1910 it had annexed Korea, taken Taiwan from China and taken southern Sakhalin (Karafuto) from Russia. After the 1914–18 war it took over, under a League of Nations mandate, the Caroline, Mariana and Marshall islands, which had been German colonies.

In 1931 the Japanese occupied Manchuria (the north-eastern region of China), where in 1932 they established a puppet state called Manchukuo. During the 1930s they conquered a large part of eastern China. In 1940 they moved into French Indochina (now Vietnam, Laos and Cambodia). In 1941 they occupied Thailand, and, in a sweeping attack on all the American, British and Dutch territories in the Far East, Japanese forces were by mid-1942 in control of the Philippines, Guam and Wake Island; Hong Kong, Malaya, Singapore, British Borneo and most of Burma; all the Dutch East Indies (now Indonesia); much of New Guinea, most of the Solomons and all the Gilbert Islands, and, far to the north, the western Aleutians.

All these conquests were wiped out in 1945. China recovered Taiwan. The USSR (which had joined in the war against Japan only a few days before it surrendered) recovered southern Sakhalin, seized the Kurile islands and occupied Manchuria and North Korea until local communities had got a grip on those territories (53, 58). American forces occupied South Korea (until 1949) and the Ryukyu and Bonin islands, as well as Japan itself, where Commonwealth troops joined them.

In the peace treaty concluded in 1951 with all the victorious allies of 1945 except China and the USSR, Japan renounces its claims on Taiwan, Korea, Sakhalin and the Caroline, Mariana and Marshall islands. The allied occupation of Japan was ended; Japan concluded a mutual security treaty with the United States and gave it the right to keep forces in Japan for joint defence.

The Carolines, Marianas and Marshalls became the American-administered Trust Territory of the Pacific Islands (often, for short, called Micronesia, 66). Between 1953 and 1972 the Americans returned to Japanese control, group by group, the Bonins, the adjacent Volcano Islands

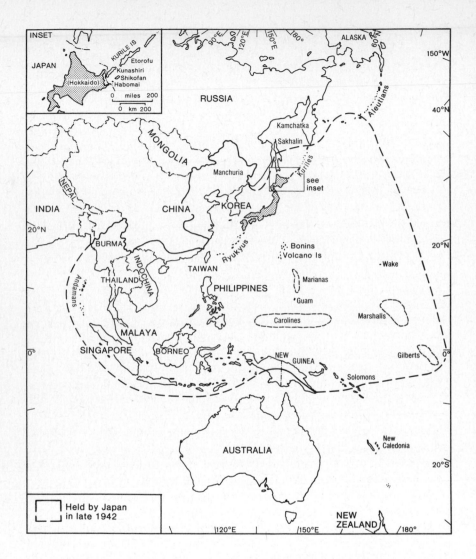

INSET

JAPAN

(Hokkaido)

KURILE IS
Etorofu
Kunashiri
Shikofan
Habomai

0   miles   200
0   km   200

RUSSIA

ALASKA

150°W

40°N

Kamchatka

Sakhalin

Aleutians

MONGOLIA

Manchuria

Kuriles

see
inset

NEPAL

INDIA

CHINA

KOREA

20°N

20°N

BURMA

Ryukyus

Bonins
Volcano Is

Wake

20°N

INDOCHINA

THAILAND

TAIWAN

Marianas

Andamans

PHILIPPINES

Guam

MALAYA

Carolines

Marshalls

SINGAPORE

BORNEO

0°

NEW
GUINEA

Gilberts

0°

Solomons

AUSTRALIA

New
Caledonia

20°S

Held by Japan
in late 1942

NEW
ZEALAND

120°E

150°E

180°

(including Iwojima) and the northern and southern Ryukyus (including Okinawa, where the USA retained rights to a base).

In 1978 Japan was at last able to conclude a peace treaty with China. It had signed no peace treaty with the USSR, largely because of a continuing dispute over the Habomai, Shikotan, Kunashiri and Etorofu (Iturup) islands, which lie near Hokkaido, the northernmost of Japan's main islands. The USSR seized these islands in 1945, along with the rest of the

Kuriles chain, and in 1990 it was still rejecting Japanese calls for their return – although its growing need for Japanese economic help suggested that a deal might soon be done.

Japan's brief but spectacular phase of territorial conquest had been spurred on by the belief that a populous island nation, with few minerals and only limited farmland, must acquire overseas 'living space' and sources of raw materials. It was the oil, rubber, tin, iron ore and other minerals of South-East Asia that Japan's armed forces went south to seize in 1941–2. Yet it was after 1945, when Japan was forced back to its pre-1895 territory, that it developed its economy so successfully that it became a superpower in economic terms.

It has effectively curbed its population growth, and this has contributed to its high standard of living. It still depends heavily on oil imported mainly from the Middle East and on imports of minerals from various countries, including Australia, Canada, India and South Africa. But its industrial strength and importance as a market for countries that export raw materials have gained it a position of great influence in the Far East and Pacific regions, and maintained it in that position far longer than its armies ever did. And, after failing to defeat Americans and Europeans in war, it has bested them in peace – building up huge surpluses in its trade with the United States, and acquiring (especially in the 1980s) large industrial investments there and in Europe; and also playing a powerful role in international finance (seven of the world's ten biggest banks are Japanese).

58 Korea

Korea's history has largely been a story of Chinese, Japanese and Russian contests for supremacy. For centuries China claimed Korea as a vassal state, but by the 1890s Japan and Russia were struggling to control it, and Japan seized it after defeating Russia in their 1904–5 war (57).

When Japan surrendered in 1945 the USSR occupied northern Korea (north of 38° North) and American forces occupied the south. The USSR agreed, in theory, to help to establish a united and democratic Korea, but in practice it installed a communist regime in the north, suppressing all opposition. Elections were then held in South Korea, which has two-thirds of the total population (now about 64 million), and a government was set up in Seoul. The American and Soviet forces both withdrew.

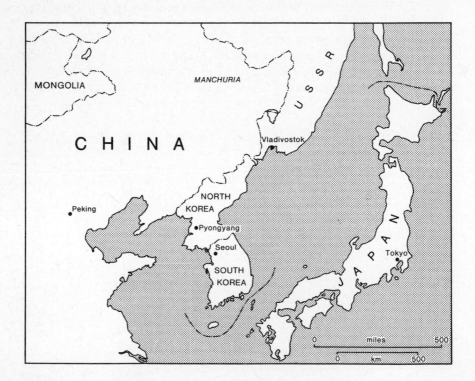

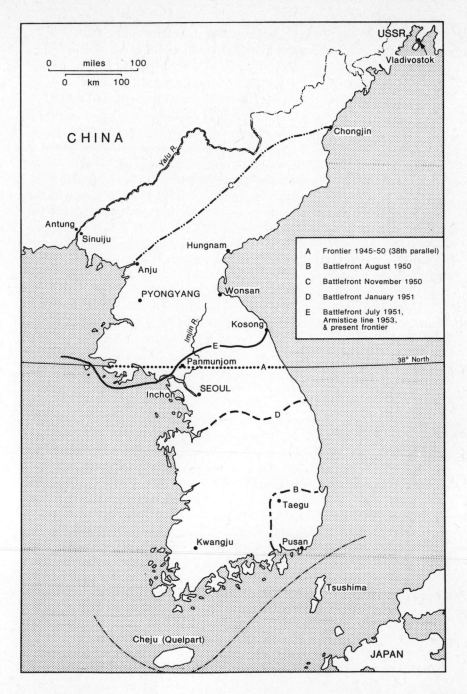

A   Frontier 1945-50 (38th parallel)

B   Battlefront August 1950

C   Battlefront November 1950

D   Battlefront January 1951

E   Battlefront July 1951,
    Armistice line 1953,
    & present frontier

CHINA

USSR
Vladivostok

Chongjin

Antung
Sinuiju

Hungnam

Anju

PYONGYANG
Wonsan

Kosong

Imjin R.

E

Panmunjom   A   38° North

SEOUL

Inchon

D

B
Taegu

Kwangju   Pusan

Tsushima

Cheju (Quelpart)

JAPAN

0   miles   100

0   km   100

Yalu R.

In June 1950 North Korea, which had been heavily armed by the USSR, invaded the south, capturing Seoul within a few days. American troops were sent to help resist the invasion; the UN Security Council urged other nations to help (the USSR was then boycotting the council's meetings, so it did not veto this move, *8*), and altogether 16 nations sent men to fight in Korea under the UN flag. But at first only a few US and Commonwealth units could get there, and they and the South Koreans were forced back to the area around Pusan. In September, however, fresh US forces landed at Inchon and cut the communist army's supply lines. The North Koreans were driven back across the thirty-eighth parallel, but they refused to make peace. The UN forces advanced into the north; when they neared the Chinese frontier, China sent into Korea a large army which drove south so far that Seoul fell into communist hands once again. By June 1951 the allies had fought their way north of the thirty-eighth parallel again, China's army had suffered huge losses, and it agreed to start talks. The talks, held mainly at Panmunjom, dragged on until 1953, when (after Stalin's death) an armistice was signed.

A peace conference at Geneva in 1954 became deadlocked, and Korea remained divided along the 1953 armistice line. After the quarrel between China and the USSR in the 1960s, North Korea sought to become 'neutral' as between them; it thus got some support from each of them for its policy of maintaining military pressure on South Korea. This pressure led to South Korea, too, to maintain strong armed forces, which came to dominate its politics; from 1963 onward its presidents were all generals.

South Korea prospered; within 30 years income per head had risen from a level much like India's to one close to Spain's or Greece's. Impatience with military rule produced a revolt at Kwangju in 1980 and then, in 1987, constitutional reforms under which a new president and legislature were elected. Meanwhile North Korea's communist rulers kept it sealed off from the outside world, and very poor. They felt betrayed when Chinese and Soviet athletes were sent to South Korea to take part in the 1988 Olympic Games in Seoul; and more so in 1990, when diplomatic relations were established between South Korea and the USSR, while North Korea was told not to expect any more Soviet or Chinese economic aid. Reluctantly the northern regime agreed to start high-level talks with South Korea.

59 South-East Asia

Before the 1939–45 war the only independent nation in South-East Asia was Thailand (called Siam until the 1930s). The rest of the region was under European or American rule: French in Indochina (Vietnam, Laos and Cambodia); Dutch in the East Indies (now Indonesia); British in Burma, Malaya and northern Borneo; American in the Philippines. The Japanese moved into Indochina in 1940 and overran the whole region in 1941–2 (57). In 1945 the Dutch were unable to regain full control of Indonesia, which later became an independent nation (63). The United States gave independence to the Philippines in 1946; Britain gave it to Burma in 1948, to Malaya in 1957 (52, 62, 66). In Indochina, France faced a communist-led Vietnamese independence movement which, after the communists' victory in China's civil war, received strong support from China (54, 60).

By 1954 North Vietnam was being taken over by a communist regime which was also gaining footholds in Laos, Cambodia and South Vietnam. Communist guerrilla forces were active in Burma, Malaya and the Philippines, and there was anxiety about the new strong China's influence on the region's large Chinese communities (there are now about 40 million Chinese in South-East Asia). Thailand and the Philippines joined Australia, Britain, France, New Zealand, Pakistan and the United States in signing the 1954 Manila treaty on South-East Asian defence, often called SEATO. These allies agreed to act together against any attack in the region on one of them or on Cambodia, Laos or South Vietnam, although action on the territory on one of those three states would require its consent.

No joint defence action was taken under SEATO's formal authority, although American, Australian, New Zealand, Philippine and Thai forces went to fight in Vietnam in the 1960s (60). In the 1970s SEATO's activities were ended. Much had changed in the region. In Indochina military victory had gone to the communists, but Vietnam's communist rulers broke with China after 1975, siding with the USSR against it and initiating a new quarrel over Cambodia (61). Meanwhile a new grouping, more truly regional than SEATO, had been formed.

The Association of South-East Asian Nations (ASEAN) was formed in 1967 by Indonesia, Malaysia, the Philippines, Singapore and Thailand; Brunei (62) joined them in 1984. It was not a military alliance; Thailand

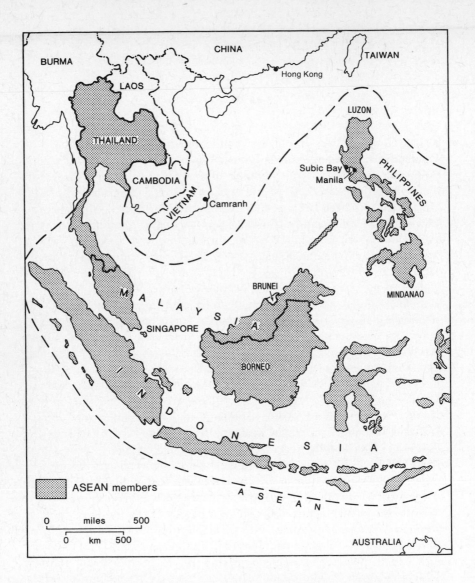

BURMA

CHINA

TAIWAN

LAOS

Hong Kong

THAILAND

CAMBODIA

LUZON

PHILIPPINES

Subic Bay
Manila

VIETNAM

Camranh

MALAYSIA

BRUNEI

MINDANAO

SINGAPORE

BORNEO

INDONESIA

ASEAN

ASEAN members

| 0 | miles | 500 |

| 0 | km | 500 |

AUSTRALIA

and the Philippines kept some defence links with the USA (*66*). But the ASEAN states worked together quite effectively for certain purposes; for example, they prevented the regime that Vietnam had installed in Cambodia from taking over the Cambodian seat at the United Nations. In the 1980s the Philippines still faced continuing activity by communist guerrillas – as well as sporadic Moro (Muslim) rebellion in Mindanao – which did not end when a bloodless revolution ousted the notoriously corrupt regime of President Marcos in 1986. The new government began negotiations about the future of the US bases in the Philippines, including the Subic Bay naval base, whose importance had been increased by the USSR's acquisition in 1975 of a naval base at Camranh in Vietnam. This problem was eased in 1990 when the US accepted Singapore's offer of naval facilities (62).

A new problem for the whole region had emerged in 1975 when huge numbers of people began trying to escape from the three Indochina states, now all under communist rule; by the end of the 1980s more than 2 million had got out. Cambodian refugees mostly crossed the frontier into Thailand, but many of the far more numerous refugees from Vietnam got out by sea in small craft. Those 'boat people' who survived these hazardous journeys found only temporary refuge in the ASEAN countries, which had to be reassured that they would be resettled elsewhere. By 1990 the United States had accepted about 900,000; Australia, Canada, and France, about 125,000 each; a dozen other countries, much smaller numbers. Special problems arose over 'boat people' who reached Hong Kong – a crowded place already struggling to avoid being swamped by new waves of Chinese trying to get across the frontier from the mainland (56).

An older regional problem is the large-scale production of opium from poppies grown in Burma's Shan hills and the adjacent border areas of China, Laos, Vietnam and Thailand (52). Increasingly, the opium is now made into heroin and smuggled out as such through China or Thailand. Little has been done to curb this drug trafficking at source; parts of the 'Golden Triangle' borderland are not effectively controlled by any of the governments concerned.

There have been few territorial disputes among the ASEAN states, although Malaysia and the Philippines both have claims on the Spratly islands (54) and the two have at times been at odds over an old Philippines claim to Sabah (62). The ASEAN six have often worked as a team; for example, in meetings with European Community ministers. In 1989 the six joined Australia, Canada, Japan, South Korea, New Zealand and the United States to create the Asia and Pacific Economic Co-operation Council (APEC).

60 Indochina

Cambodia, Laos and Vietnam (Annam) all came under French rule between 1860 and 1900, forming French Indochina. During the 1940–5 Japanese occupation the communist-led Vietminh independence movement launched a guerrilla war in northern Vietnam (Tongking, or Tonkin), and in 1945 it set up a government in Hanoi. Fighting between the French and the Vietminh followed, while France began a transfer of power to non-communist governments in Cambodia and Laos as well as in Vietnam. In 1954, after the Vietminh had trapped a French force at Dien Bien Phu, cease-fire agreements were signed. Vietnam was divided at the 17° North parallel. The French withdrew from North Vietnam, where the Vietminh again installed a government in Hanoi; in South Vietnam the French completed the transfer of sovereignty to the government in Saigon. About 800,000 Vietnamese fled from north to south.

France also withdrew its forces from Cambodia and Laos, whose governments now had full sovereignty. In Laos attempts were made to include the communists in a coalition government, but clashes multiplied, and by 1961 the capital, Vientiane, was threatened by advancing communist troops. A new coalition was installed after a 1962 conference at Geneva, but confused struggles were soon resumed. Weak governments in Laos and Cambodia could not prevent their eastern border areas being used by the North Vietnamese to move troops and arms south (along the 'Ho Chi Minh trail') and infiltrate them into South Vietnam from the west.

By the early 1960s South Vietnam's government was losing control of many rural areas to guerrillas who were supplied, reinforced and directed from North Vietnam. The Americans, who since 1954 had given South Vietnam large-scale aid in the hope of checking the southward advance of communist power, became more directly involved in the struggle. In 1961 US 'combat advisers' were operating with South Vietnamese units; by 1963 there were 16,000 US military personnel in Vietnam; in 1965 US aircraft began to bombard North Vietnam, and US ground forces arrived in the south; by 1968 there were 500,000 Americans there – and, alongside them and the South Vietnamese troops, there were contingents from Australia, New Zealand, the Philippines, South Korea and Thailand.

The Hanoi government's response to offers of peace showed that it

C H I N A

Caobang

Laocai

Red River

Langson

Dien Bien Phu

HANOI

Mekong

Luang Prabang

River

Gulf of Tongking

Hainan (China)

Vientiane

VIETNAM

Udon Thani

17° North

Savannakhet

Hué

THAILAND

LAOS

Danang

Ubon

Mekong R.

Kontum

BANGKOK

CAMBODIA

Battambang

Tonle Sap Lake

Dalat

Camranh

PHNOM PENH

Kompong Som

SAIGON (Ho Chi Minh City)

Mekong Delta

0   miles   150

0   km   150

would accept nothing short of a communist take-over of South Vietnam; and this, in due course, it achieved. In 1969 the withdrawal of the US and allied forces began. In 1973 it was completed. A cease-fire was announced, but fighting soon became widespread again. During 1974 the North Vietnamese army fighting in the south became as large as South Vietnam's. By 1975 it was larger, and, advancing from the border areas which it had entered mainly by way of Laos and Cambodia, it captured Saigon and other southern cities. The forcible uniting of Vietnam under communist rule also meant rule by northerners. Saigon was renamed Ho Chi Minh City; southern communists were allowed little power; southern non-communists were hunted down, and a new refugee tide was set in motion (59).

After the fall of Saigon, Laos was quickly taken over by communist forces which, from the start, were effectively controlled by North Vietnam. In Cambodia, however, the communist Khmer Rouge who captured Phnom Penh in 1975 were soon in dispute with Hanoi. They looked for help to China, which was becoming uneasy about having a Soviet-backed Vietnam, heavily militarized and with expansionist aims, as a neighbour. When Vietnam invaded Cambodia at the end of 1978 China hit back, staging a limited invasion of Vietnam early in 1979 (but withdrawing its troops a few weeks later, when they had captured some border towns but suffered heavy losses).

The occupation of Cambodia completed the conversion of Indochina into a Soviet sphere of influence. A special gain was that the Soviet fleet could now use a base at Camranh. This increased its capacity in the Indian Ocean as well as in the Far East (41, 59). However, by the late 1980s the USSR, which was improving its relations with both the USA and China, began to see Indochina as more of a liability than an asset. It cut down its economic aid to Vietnam, reproaching Vietnam's rulers for mishandling the economy and failing to initiate reforms. Those rulers, for their part, were alarmed by the sight of political changes in the USSR and eastern Europe, and they began, at last, to seek better relations with China, whose fierce suppression of dissent in 1989 had found approval in Hanoi's rigidly doctrinaire ruling circles.

61 Cambodia

Cambodia (Kampuchea) is the remnant of the old Khmer kingdom which once included the Mekong delta. Later, Cambodia was dominated by Vietnam during several periods before becoming a French protectorate in 1863. Unlike Laos, it has no border mountains separating it from Vietnam, and there are traditions of antagonism between the two. In 1954 Cambodia became independent. In the 1960s it kept out of the Vietnam fighting by turning a blind eye to North Vietnam's use of the 'Ho Chi Minh trail' across Cambodian territory (60); but in 1970 Cambodia itself became a battlefield. The communist guerrillas (Khmer Rouge) got the upper hand when American support for the government was withdrawn, and they captured Phnom Penh in 1975 (two weeks before the fall of Saigon).

Cambodia's new communist rulers quickly became notorious for their ineptness and cruelty. They drove out the cities' inhabitants, ordering everybody to work in the fields; the result was mass starvation, and a flood of refugees into Thailand. The Khmer Rouge refused to follow Vietnam in toeing the Soviet line; they turned to China, hoping it would shield them from Vietnamese pressure. In 1978, after many border clashes, Vietnam's forces launched a full-scale invasion. In 1979 they captured Phnom Penh and installed a puppet government, led by dissident Khmer Rouge. A Vietnamese army of occupation, 150,000 strong, was deployed to hold the country down. More refugees poured into Thailand; throughout the 1980s there were about 300,000 there, mostly in camps near the frontier.

The Vietnamese troops encountered three resistance movements: two were non-communist groups, headed by pre-1975 political leaders; the third, and strongest, was run by the Khmer Rouge. In 1982 the three movements announced their formation of a coalition government. It did not control such territory inside Cambodia, and its three components were often at odds, but it got a good deal of backing in South-East Asia and beyond. (Most states refused to recognize the Cambodian government installed by Vietnam.) At first, guerrilla activity was mostly along the Thai frontier.

In the mid-1980s the USSR, anxious to conciliate China, began to press Vietnam to pull its troops out of Cambodia. Vietnam, with a mishandled economy fast deteriorating, could not maintain its army of occupation once

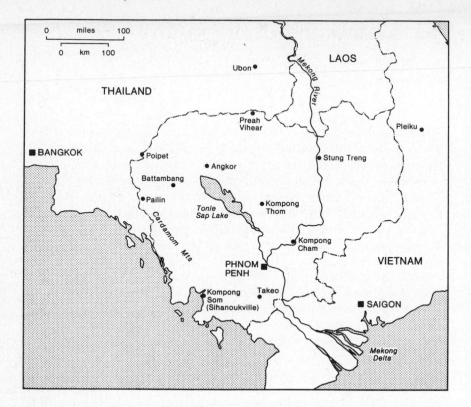

its Soviet subsidies were cut back; nor could it hope for western economic aid until its troops left Cambodia. In 1989 it withdrew all its regular forces (but some of its soldiers stayed on, wearing Cambodian uniforms). The guerrillas began to advance; in 1990 there was fighting around Battambang and Kompong Thom and in the Cardamom Mountains. Meanwhile a long series of peace talks, held in Indonesia, France and elsewhere, had been arranged. At the United Nations the Security Council's five permanent members (Britain, China, France, USA, USSR) had jointly drafted proposals for a UN peacekeeping force to disarm and disband all the warring forces in Cambodia and then supervise a free election. There were signs that China was pressing the Khmer Rouge to compromise just as hard as the USSR was pressing Vietnam and its clients in Phnom Penh.

62 Malaysia and Singapore

Malaysia, with its federal capital at Kuala Lumpur, comprises the sultanates of mainland Malaya (with Penang island) and the Borneo states of Sabah (formerly British North Borneo) and Sarawak. Five-sixths of its 16 million inhabitants live on the mainland. The majority are Malays (mostly Muslims), but about 33% are Chinese and 9% Indians; in the Borneo states there are other minorities.

Malaya (the mainland) became an independent federation in 1957, after a long period of British rule interrupted by the Japanese occupation in 1942–5. A guerrilla and terrorist campaign launched by communist Chinese in Malaya in 1948 was not completely defeated until 1960, but democratic elections were held regularly from 1955 onward, producing federal governments based on a Malay-led alliance that included Chinese and Indian parties. Although rifts emerged within this alliance, it continued to win elections in the 1980s, fighting off Malay politicians who invoked Islamic fundamentalism (28) and tried to exploit Malay resentment of the wealth of some Chinese.

Singapore, an island of only 225 square miles, developed during 140 years of British rule into a major port, with a British naval base until 1971. It now has 2.7 million inhabitants, 76% of them Chinese, 15% Malay and 7% Indian. In 1963, together with Sabah and Sarawak, it joined Malaya in the enlarged federation, renamed Malaysia. But the mainland Malays were not happy about taking this large Chinese element into the federation. In 1965 Singapore was obliged to withdraw, and it became a separate independent republic. By the 1980s, having adapted swiftly to the new high-technology era in industry, it had raised its income per head to a level higher than Spain's. In 1990 it made an agreement with the United States providing for American naval and other facilities in Singapore (59).

In 1963 the inclusion of Sabah and Sarawak in Malaysia had been angrily opposed by Indonesia, even after UN investigations had confirmed that their inhabitants wanted to join the federation. The campaign of 'confrontation' launched by Indonesia included armed raids across the frontier in Borneo, and even on mainland Malaya. These were repelled with the help of British forces, and in 1965, after a new government had come to power in Indonesia, it abandoned the campaign. In the 1960s the Philip-

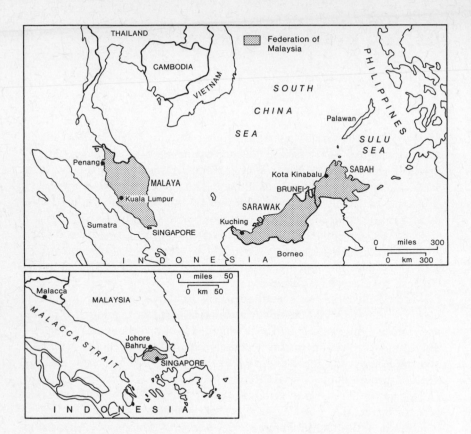

pines briefly revived an old claim to Sabah, and during the 1980s Malaysia and the Philippines asserted claims to parts of the Spratly group (54).

The sultanate of Brunei in north Borneo chose not to join Malaysia in 1963, and remained under British protection until it became fully independent in 1984, with the formal name of Brunei Darussalam. With a population of only 230,000, Brunei was formerly distinguished by its possession of a rich oilfield; but more recently offshore discoveries have made Malaysia also an oil exporter.

63 Indonesia and New Guinea

In 1945 Holland was unable to restore its authority over the Dutch East Indies, which Japan had seized in 1942. An independent republic, initially controlling only some parts of Java and Sumatra, was proclaimed. Its leaders negotiated with the Dutch, but in 1947 fighting became widespread. The United Nations obtained a cease-fire, sent military observers and helped to get an agreed transfer of sovereignty in 1949. The new independent Indonesia included all the former Dutch territory except the western half of New Guinea (now Irian Jaya, but then usually called West Irian), whose Melanesian inhabitants had nothing in common with the mainly Muslim, Malay-speaking Indonesians.

Indonesia pressed its demands for West Irian; in 1962 its forces began to attack the territory, and the Dutch agreed to transfer it. A temporary UN administration, backed by a UN force, eased the transition, and Indonesian rule began in 1963. It had been agreed that the 800,000 inhabitants should be asked by 1969 whether they accepted Indonesian rule. There were risings in 1969, and many people fled into eastern New Guinea; but Indonesia produced some show of support by groups supposedly representing the territory's people.

Of Indonesia's 185 million people, 60% are crowded into Java. Relations between the various islands have at times been strained – partly by the government's projects for resettling Javanese in other regions. One local problem has been that of Ambon (Amboina) and the neighbouring South Moluccan islands, one of the earliest areas of European colonization. Thousands of Christian Ambonese emigrated to Holland after 1949, and some groups continued to demand separate independence for the South Moluccas. A more widespread problem is that of Indonesia's Chinese minority (about 3%), who have sometimes served as scapegoats in times of trouble. When the army seized power in 1965 it accused many Chinese of involvement in a communist plot; relations with (communist) China, which had become very close under the previous regime, were broken off – and not formally restored until 1990.

Before the 1965 coup, Indonesia had been trying to prevent the formerly British parts of Borneo from joining the Malaysian federation (62). In 1975 Indonesia seized East Timor, the only part of the East Indies that Portugal

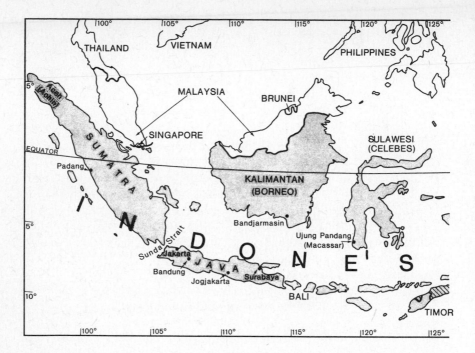

had retained when it lost control of the region to the Dutch in the seventeenth century. When the end of Portuguese rule seemed imminent (27), pro-Indonesian groups in East Timor had started fighting those who wanted independence. Indonesia's forces suppressed the independence movement, Fretilin, with a brutality that alienated more of the Timorese, causing further resistance. East Timor was officially renamed Loro Sae.

Papua New Guinea (the eastern half of New Guinea, with the adjacent islands) became independent in 1975. Previously, its southern part (the Territory of Papua) was an Australian dependency, and the north – with the islands, including Bougainville in the northern Solomons – was an Australian-administered UN trust territory. (It had been held by Germany from 1884 to 1914, and occupied by Japan from 1942 to 1944.

There have been separatist agitations in Bougainville, where in 1988 rebel groups closed down a big copper mine, cutting PNG's exports by a third. A different problem has sometimes arisen from border-crossings by Indonesian forces in pursuit of guerrillas who were still resisting Indonesian rule in Irian Jaya (western New Guinea). In the 1980s thousands of refugees from Irian Jaya fled across the long land frontier, which PNG's

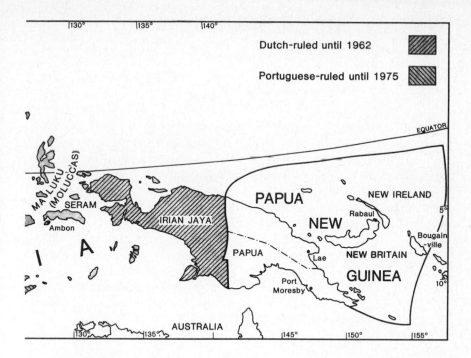

small armed forces could not control; its people, moreover, felt some natural sympathy for their western neighbours, who in many cases were their kinsfolk. By contrast, soldiers sent by PNG were able, in 1980, to give decisive help to newly independent Vanuatu by ending the secessionist rebellion on Espiritu Santo island. This action and others have shown how Papua New Guinea, although overshadowed by its big neighbour Indonesia on one side, may now loom large in relation to its small fellow Melanesian neighbour states on the other (65).

64 Australia and New Zealand

These two nations, separated by 1,000 miles of the Tasman Sea, are isolated but also shielded by wide oceans on three sides. Mainly peopled from Britain, they at first relied on British naval protection; in 1914 and again in 1939 they rallied to Britain's side in war, sending troops to fight in Europe and the Middle East. But in 1942 they themselves faced a threat from the north: Japan's advancing forces were not stopped until they had reached New Guinea and the Solomon Islands.

Australia and New Zealand made a defence treaty with the United States (ANZUS) in 1951, signed the SEATO treaty in 1954, and sent forces to Korea and Malaya in the 1950s and to Vietnam in the 1960s (58–60, 66). But New Zealand's 1984 election brought in a government whose 'anti-nuclear' policy led it to bar US warships from entering its ports; this ended its active participation in ANZUS.

In 1985 French secret agents sank, in Auckland harbour, a ship which an anti-nuclear group had planned to take to French Polynesia to impede test explosions at Mururoa (10). Two of the team of agents were caught, and France further angered New Zealand by breaking promises it had given to obtain their release.

Most of the 17 million Australians are townspeople; half of them live in the five biggest cities, which are all on the coast of this huge country (or

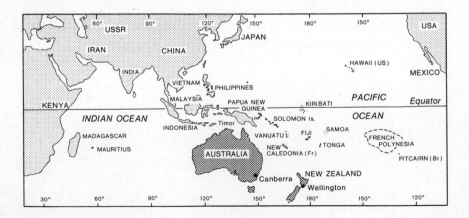

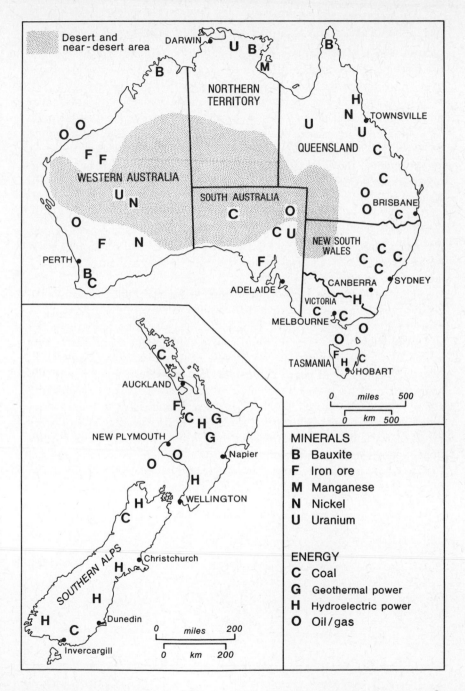

Desert and near-desert area

DARWIN

U B
M

B

NORTHERN TERRITORY

B

O O

H
N TOWNSVILLE

F F

U

QUEENSLAND

WESTERN AUSTRALIA

U N

SOUTH AUSTRALIA

C

C

O F N

C

O

O O BRISBANE

O

PERTH

B C

F

C U

NEW SOUTH WALES

C

C C C

ADELAIDE

CANBERRA

H

SYDNEY

VICTORIA

MELBOURNE

C C
O

O

TASMANIA

H H C

HOBART

0   miles   500

0   km   500

AUCKLAND

C

F

C H G

NEW PLYMOUTH

G

O O Napier

H

WELLINGTON

H

C

SOUTHERN ALPS

H

Christchurch

H

H

Dunedin

C

Invercargill

0   miles   200

0   km   200

MINERALS

B Bauxite
F Iron ore
M Manganese
N Nickel
U Uranium

ENERGY

C Coal
G Geothermal power
H Hydroelectric power
O Oil/gas

continent). A formerly pastoral economy has been transformed, particularly by discoveries of great mineral wealth (5). Minerals not marked on the map include copper, gold, tin and tungsten. Australia is a prominent exporter of aluminium, coal, iron ore and uranium.

New Zealand has not enjoyed such a mining bonanza. Its wool, meat and butter still make up two-fifths of its exports. However, two-thirds of its 3.5 million inhabitants now live in the main urban areas. It had to struggle to diversify its overseas trade when Britain, which used to take 70% of its exports, joined the European Community (19), whose protectionist farm policies had the effect of slashing sales of New Zealand meat and butter to Britain. Its biggest markets are now Australia, Japan and the USA.

The 1965 New Zealand–Australia Free Trade Agreement (NAFTA) was mainly aimed at reducing tariffs on trade across the Tasman Sea. In 1982 the two countries completed a CER ('closer economic relations') pact, under which nearly all restrictions on trade between them were to be removed by stages.

Since the ending in 1973 of the 'White Australia' policy, Asians have come to make up a third of Australia's annual intake of immigrants; it has taken in about 125,000 refugees from Vietnam (59). On current trends the population should reach 25 million by 2030. Only about 1% of Australians are of Aboriginal descent; but 12% of New Zealanders are at least partly of Maori (Polynesian) origin. In the 1980s Maori tribes, appealing to the terms of the 1840 Treaty of Waitangi, launched a campaign to obtain the return of, or compensation for, land and sea fishing rights lost since 1840. There has also been much recent immigration into New Zealand of other Polynesian islanders, especially from the Cook Islands and Niue, former dependencies still in association with New Zealand, and Western Samoa, a former UN trust territory now fully independent (8, 65). In Auckland, the biggest New Zealand city, a third of the inhabitants are Polynesian.

65 South Pacific

By 1980 tiny Pitcairn was the only British dependency in the region. Since 1970 Fiji, Kiribati, the Solomon Islands, Tonga and Tuvalu had become independent (9). Kiribati and Tuvalu were formerly the Gilbert and Ellice Islands. Banaba (Ocean Island) was included in Kiribati after long negotiations with the 2,000 Banabans, who had sought separate independence.

French Polynesia, New Caledonia, and Wallis and Futuna remained French overseas territories. Melanesian pressure for independence had mounted in New Caledonia, but its Kanaks (Melanesians) now form only 43% of its population. Partly because it has become a major source of nickel (5), it has a European minority of about 37%; the other inhabitants have come from other Pacific islands or from Asia. In the 1980s changes of government in France produced a series of new constitutional arrangements for the island, where, at times, unrest took violent forms.

In 1980 the British–French condominium of the New Hebrides became independent as Vanuatu. It called in troops from Papua New Guinea (63) to help suppress a secessionist revolt on Espiritu Santo island. Nauru and Western Samoa, formerly UN trust territories administered respectively by Australia and New Zealand (8, 9), are now independent. The Cook Islands and Niue are self-governing in association with New Zealand; the Tokelaus are a New Zealand territory (64).

The region's biggest concentration of population is in Fiji – about 700,000, half of them descended from immigrants who came from India a century ago. Although outnumbered, the Fijians have retained political control. When the 1987 election brought an Indian-led government to power, the army took over; a republic was declared, and a new constitution imposed which ensured continuing Fijian dominance. Fiji's Commonwealth membership was suspended because of this overt racial discrimination (9).

Under the generally accepted new law of the sea (6), even small island states can now claim large sea areas and charge foreigners for the right to fish in them. These islands states have few other resources. Since 1971 they have met regularly with Australia and New Zealand in the South Pacific Forum. In 1980 its members signed a regional trade and economic co-operation agreement (SPARTECA) that gives island products favoured

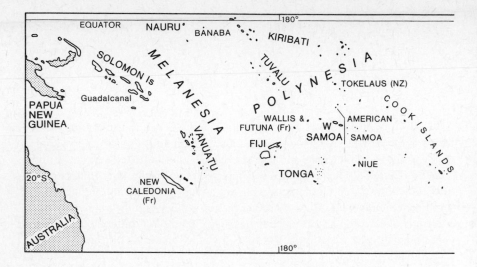

access to the Australian and New Zealand markets. Forum members have urged France to stop staging nuclear tests at Mururoa (*10*). In 1985 they concluded a treaty designating the South Pacific a 'nuclear-free zone' but leaving open the question of nuclear-armed or nuclear-powered ships' movements, over which New Zealand was in dispute with the USA (*64*).

North of the equator, but near enough to it to be often called 'South Pacific' islands, are the Carolines, Marianas and Marshalls, once held by Germany, then by Japan (*57*), and then, after 1947, an American-administered 'strategic' UN trust territory (*66*), sometimes called Micronesia. During the 1980s the trusteeship was terminated and, in a series of referendums, the northern Marianas chose to become a commonwealth linked with the US in a relationship similar to Puerto Rico's (*71*), while the Marshalls, the Federated States of Micronesia (most of the Carolines) and Palau (the Carolines' westernmost group) voted for free association with the US. The Americans retained the right to use some defence facilities in the islands, and were to continue to provide economic aid for their inhabitants, who total about 175,000.

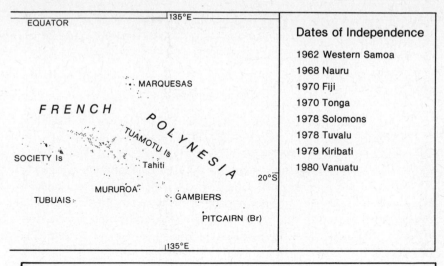

EQUATOR — 135°E —

MARQUESAS

F R E N C H   P O L Y N E S I A

TUAMOTU Is

SOCIETY Is

Tahiti

20°S

MURUROA   GAMBIERS

TUBUAIS

PITCAIRN (Br)

135°E

Dates of Independence

1962 Western Samoa
1968 Nauru
1970 Fiji
1970 Tonga
1978 Solomons
1978 Tuvalu
1979 Kiribati
1980 Vanuatu

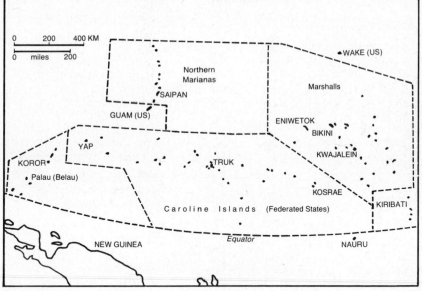

| 0 | 200 | 400 KM |
| 0 | miles | 200 |

WAKE (US)

Northern
Marianas

Marshalls

SAIPAN

GUAM (US)

ENIWETOK

BIKINI

YAP

KWAJALEIN

KOROR

TRUK

Palau (Belau)

KOSRAE

KIRIBATI

Caroline Islands (Federated States)

NEW GUINEA

Equator

NAURU

193

66 America and the Pacific

In the nineteenth century the Americans reached out into the Pacific. They bought Alaska from the Russians (1867), took the Philippines and Guam from Spain (1898), and annexed Midway, Hawaii, Wake and eastern Samoa. Between 1904 and 1914 they built the Panama Canal (6, 70), giving ships a far shorter route between Atlantic and Pacific than the ones through the Magellan strait or around Cape Horn (72, 73). In Japan, whose rulers had long rebuffed all foreign contact, the Americans' opening up of the country to trade (1854) had fateful consequences; later they became alarmed by

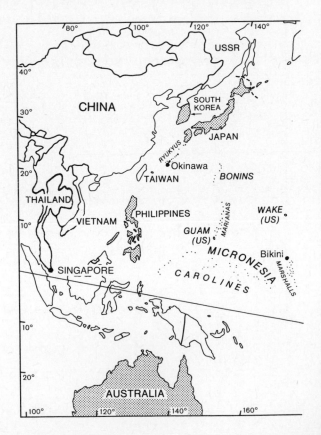

Japan's ambitions – which eventually led to its 1941 attack on the US naval base at Pearl Harbor, on Oahu island in the Hawaiian group. Japan then seized the Philippines, Guam, Wake and the westernmost Aleutians (57).

After the Americans had fought their way back across the Pacific and forced Japan to surrender in 1945, they became committed to protecting areas along the ocean's western shores. In the 1950s the invasion of South Korea and the communist forces' advances in Indochina aroused fears about the new power of a China which then had Soviet backing. The Americans undertook to protect Taiwan against attack from the Chinese mainland, and South Korea against any renewed attack from the north, and they were gradually drawn into the conflict in Vietnam (55, 58–60).

In 1951 they joined Australia and New Zealand in the ANZUS treaty (64), and signed another treaty with Japan (57). In 1954 the ANZUS allies, with Britain, France, Pakistan, the Philippines and Thailand, signed the

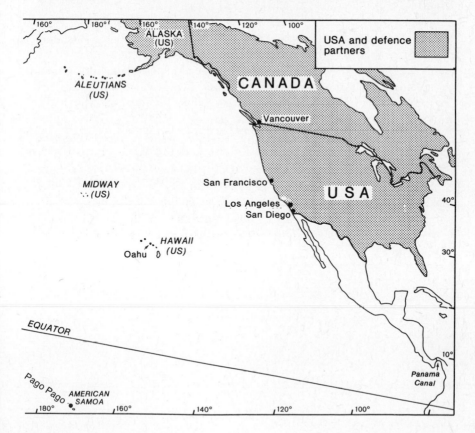

SEATO treaty (59); during the 1970s SEATO activity ended and the US bases in Thailand were closed, but there were still US bases in the Philippines, and Pakistan obtained new US military aid after the Soviet invasion of Afghanistan (49). During the 1960s and 1970s the whole situation in the Pacific regions was changed by the rift between China and the USSR, the American *rapprochement* with China, the communists' military victories in Indochina and the bitter feelings that the war in Vietnam aroused among Americans, moving them to withdraw from that struggle and recoil from the idea of involvement in any similar conflict (53, 55, 60). By the end of the 1980s there were further great changes, including the huge economic advance of Japan (although Japan limited its military commitments to self-defence) and the weakening of the USSR (which, consequently, sought better relations with the US, Japan and China). In the Asia–Pacific Economic Co-operation Council (APEC), formed in 1989, Japan and the US were clearly the dominant members (2, 57, 59).

The United States had given the Philippines independence in 1946. Between 1953 and 1972 it returned the Ryukyu, Bonin and Volcano islands to Japanese control (57). Alaska and Hawaii, previously dependent territories, became the forty-ninth and fiftieth of the United States in 1959. Guam (in the southern Marianas), American Samoa, Midway and Wake are US territories. The Carolines, Marianas (excluding Guam) and Marshalls, which until the mid-1980s were a 'strategic' UN trust territory under American administration, have now chosen other forms of association with the US (65). In the 1950s Bikini and Eniwetok, in the Marshalls, had been used for US nuclear tests, and missile test firings (without warheads) have been directed at the waters near Kwajalein in the Marshalls (10). China and the USSR have also tested missiles by firing them at Pacific sea areas, and have deployed increasingly strong naval forces in the ocean; but the United States has long been predominant there in terms of conventional naval power.

67 United States of America

Originally there were only 13 states (all along the Atlantic seaboard) in the American federation. After 1912, when Arizona attained statehood, there were 48. In 1959 Alaska and Hawaii (66), formerly US territories, became the forty-ninth and fiftieth states.

Since the 1930s the population has doubled; it is now 250 million. Immigration has been running at about 1.2 million a year, half of it illegal (largely across the Mexican frontier). Although the United States was mainly peopled from Europe, and its immigration quotas were long designed to preserve the population mix, nine out of every ten recent immigrants have come from third-world countries.

The total population now includes about 23 million people of Hispanic American origin (in 1970 there were only 9 million); 6.5 million Asians (including nearly 1 million Vietnamese, 59); 2 million American Indians; and 32 million 'blacks', partly or wholly of African origin. Less than half the blacks live in the south-east (the 'Old South'), where 85% lived in the 1920s. They have moved in huge numbers to northern cities, and make up a third or more of the population of, e.g., Chicago or Detroit. (In some inner-city areas there are black majorities; the capital, Washington, is a particular example.)

But the biggest shift of balance has been towards the south and west, away from the north-east and north central (Middle West) regions, now dubbed the 'Rust Belt' because of the relative decline of their heavy industries. Since the 1970s the south and west have contained more than half the total population – so they elect more than half of the House of Representatives and have more than half the votes in presidential elections. Sophisticated industries have expanded in the southern 'Sunbelt' (income per head in the south is now 90% of the national average; in 1940 it was only 50%) and in the far west (e.g. computers in 'Silicon Valley' south-east of San Francisco, jumbo jets in Seattle). New York, the most populous state until the 1960s, has been far outstripped by California (now 30 million; in 1950, only 11 million). Of California's inhabitants, 25% are now Hispanic and 9% Asian – a measure of how immigration by those elements has helped to tilt the balance of population.

Development in the south and west has been fostered by the exploita-

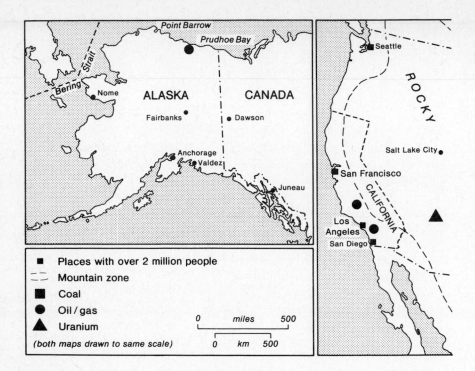

Places with over 2 million people
Mountain zone
Coal
Oil/gas
Uranium
(both maps drawn to same scale)

0   miles   500

0   km   500

tion of oil and natural gas and the building of dams (to provide both hydro-electric power and irrigation). Alaskan oil, piped to Valdez and thence moved in tankers, and oil and gas piped south from Canada have helped to reduce American dependence on oil from the Middle East; but the United States, despite its own huge output (*3*), is still a major oil importer. In the 1980s the increase in its use of nuclear energy was sharply checked by anxiety about safety, partly because of the 1979 accident at the Three Mile Island reactor in Pennsylvania, 100 miles west of Philadelphia – although this was much less serious than the catastrophe at Chernobyl in the USSR in 1986 (*4, 14*).

After the 1914–18 war 'isolationism' was strong enough to keep the United States out of the League of Nations. After the 1939–45 war, however, the headquarters of the League's successor, the United Nations, were sited in New York (*8*); as the greatest economic power, and the only military power able to match the USSR, the United States found many other countries looking to it for help and leadership (*2, 7, 10*) – but not necessarily following every lead it gave. For 45 years it has kept forces in

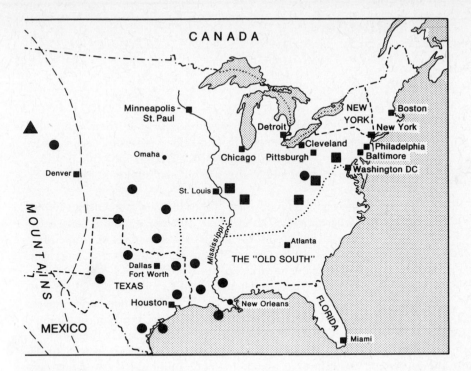

Germany, Japan and elsewhere in Europe and the Far East (*20, 66*); it has come to play a major part in the affairs of the Middle East and adjoining countries (*41–9*); more recently, it has taken a hand in some disputed issues in southern Africa (*33, 34*); and it has had to give more attention to its own 'backyard' in the Caribbean and Central American regions, where its formerly dominant position is no longer taken for granted (*69–71*). America's international involvement, from 1945 onwards, was largely a response to challenges from communist regimes in Europe and Asia. But there was no great swing back to 'isolationism' of the 1920s type, either in the later 1970s after the bitter experience of the Vietnam war (*60*), or in the later 1980s, when the collapse of communism in eastern Europe (*13, 16*) did not immediately produce a mood of triumphant complacency in the United States.

68 Canada

In 1982 Canada at last completed its constitution (which dated from 1867) by adopting a formula for amending it. Until then, absurdly, each change had to be formally approved by Britain – because this fully independent nation's federal government and ten provincial ones could not agree on an amending formula.

The long controversy was really part of the still unfinished debate about Canada's unity. That unity has always been a defiance of both geography and history. Nearly all the 26 million Canadians live in a 3,000-mile long strip of territory bordering the United States but, despite strong American influences, they have maintained a separate identity. Yet Canada itself is bicultural. It originated from British and French colonies, and its official languages are English and French. About 30% of the population speak French; only 44% of Canadians are of British or Irish origin, but immigrants of other origins have mostly chosen to learn and speak English.

Quebec is the only province where French Canadians are in a majority; they make up four-fifths of its population of 6.5 million. In New Brunswick they are about a third; elsewhere they make up less than 5% of the populations of Ontario (9.5 million), the four western provinces (7.5 million) and the Atlantic ones (2.25 million for the four, including New Brunswick). Some French Canadians have sought to defend French language rights throughout Canada; others, thinking that a lost cause, have argued that French culture must be defended in its one stronghold, Quebec – if necessary by separating it from Canada.

Quebec separatism was encouraged, in the late 1960s and early 1970s, by gestures from France, which strained relations between the governments in Ottawa and Paris. Provincial elections put a separatist-minded party in power in Quebec from 1976 to 1985; it was then voted out (and in a 1980 referendum it had met a setback when only half of Quebec's French-speakers backed its proposals for 'sovereignty, with association'), but the idea of separatism did not disappear. Quebec rejected the 1982 constitutional revision. That rift seemed to be healed when, at talks held at Meech Lake, north of Ottawa, in 1987, all the provinces were offered wider powers and Quebec was recognized as 'a distinct society'. But the Meech Lake deal fell through when two provinces, Manitoba and Newfoundland,

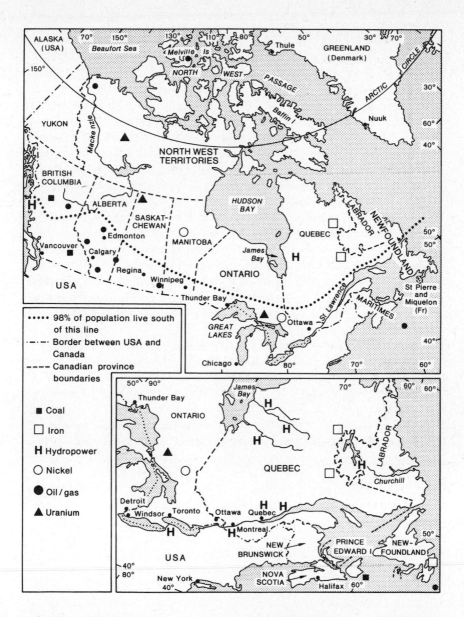

refused to ratify it by the June 1990 deadline. Opinion polls indicated that separatist feeling in Quebec was rising again.

Meanwhile, ever since federal governments began in the 1960s to worry about Quebec and to try to remedy French Canadian grievances, friction had increased between Ottawa and the western provinces, which had their own complaints against 'the east', meaning Ontario as much as Quebec. There were even some separatist rumblings in the west. And by 1990 Canada's Amerindians (2% of its population) were also pressing some of their claims more vigorously. One of the criticisms of the Meech Lake deal was that it ignored Indian and Inuit (Eskimo) rights. Plans had been drafted for a division of the huge, thinly peopled North West Territories into a western, Indian-oriented, region ('Denendeh') and an eastern, mainly Inuit, one ('Nunavut'), each with increased self-government.

In 1989, after long negotiations (and much debate among the provinces as well as in Ottawa), a free-trade agreement with the United States began to operate: tariffs on Canada–US trade (the world's biggest two-nation trade) would be abolished within ten years, and other obstacles to the flow of goods, services and investment would be reduced. Each country remained free to decide about tariffs on imports from the rest of the world. Critics of the agreement had protested that giant US firms would increase their hold on Canada's economy; its supporters stressed the need to ensure Canadian access to the vast US market at a time when US protectionist pressures were clearly growing.

Close to the coast of Newfoundland (which joined the Canadian federation as recently as 1949) lie the small islands of St Pierre and Miquelon, which are an overseas *département* of France. A long dispute between Canada and France about fishing rights in the surrounding waters began when both countries claimed 'exclusive economic zones' (EEZs) extending 200 miles from shore (6). A similar dispute between Canada and the US was resolved when the International Court at The Hague laid down a dividing line in 1984.

69 Central America, Caribbean

The United States helped Cuba to free itself from Spain in 1898, and then acquired a naval base at Guantanamo in Cuba on a lease running to 1999. It got Panama to break away from Columbia in 1903, and then built the Panama Canal (*70*). Other small ex-Spanish states in the region also became, in effect, protectorates of the US, which, until the 1930s, repeatedly sent troops to stop civil wars or restore order. Several of these states (Costa Rica being a notable exception) became notorious for oppressive military or ultra-rightist rule. In 1954 a leftist government in Guatemala was ousted by exiled rightists who, with American support, launched an invasion from Honduras and Nicaragua. In 1965 US forces intervened to stop a civil war in the Dominican Republic, but they were soon replaced by troops sent by other OAS members (*73*), which also withdrew after elections had been held.

The 1956–9 civil war in Cuba ended in victory for the forces led by Fidel Castrol, who then imposed a communist regime. A landing at the Bay of Pigs in 1961 by American-backed Cuban anti-communists was easily repelled. In 1962 the Americans detected Soviet preparations to install in Cuba nuclear missiles aimed at the US. After a tense confrontation the Soviet ships carrying the missiles to Cuba were turned back. However, Soviet aid enabled Cuba to build up strong armed forces. In the 1970s Cuban forces were sent to fight in Angola and Ethiopia (*34, 35*). Most of them had been withdrawn by the end of 1990, when Cuba was running into severe economic difficulties – partly because of mismanagement, partly because the USSR, itself in trouble (*15*), was cutting back the subsidies that had kept Castro's regime going for 30 years.

After 1959 the impact of a communist-ruled Cuba on the region was not the only cause of tension. An old frontier dispute between Honduras and El Salvador led to a war in 1969 – quickly ended by OAS mediation. Guatemala had long pressed claims to Belize (formerly British Honduras), and Guatemalan threats to seize it as soon as the British left delayed its independence until 1981. As Guatemala did not renounce its claims, Belize got Britain to leave a small force there after 1981. Britain had hoped that its Caribbean colonies could unite on their way to independence, but the West Indian Federation formed in 1958 had broken up by 1962. By 1983 12

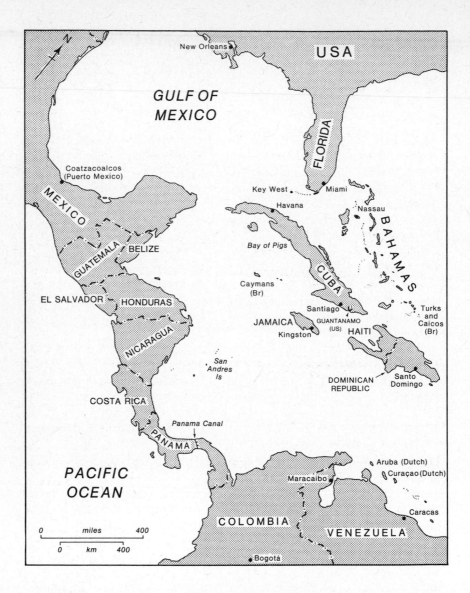

ex-British states had become independent (9, 71); they had, however, begun to co-operate through the Caribbean Community, or Caricom (73).

In Haiti the Duvalier family's 29 years of dictatorial power were ended in 1986, but the next four years saw a series of attempts to establish an elected government blocked by soldiers and policemen who still used

YUCATAN

Orange Walk

CARIBBEAN

Belize

MEXICO   PETEN   ■ BELMOPAN

MO$QUITO COAST

Trujillo

Puerto Barrias

GUATEMALA   Puerto Lempira

Solola   HONDURAS

GUATEMALA   Rio Coco

Santa   TEGUCIGALPA   Puerto
Ana   Cabezas
SAN ■   San
SALVADOR   Miguel

EL SALVADOR   Ocotal   NICARAGUA

Gulf of Fonseca   Leon

PACIFIC   MANAGUA   Bluefields

COSTA RICA

0   miles   150
0   km   150

Duvalierist methods. In Nicaragua, by contrast, the ousting in 1979 of the Somoza family, who had ruled since 1936, brought dramatic changes. During the struggle against the Somozas there had been wide support for the leftist Sandinist guerrillas (named after a rebel leader killed in 1934). Once in power, however, the Sandinist junta suppressed opposition, jailing many of its former allies, and built up such strong armed forces (with Cuban and Soviet support) that neighbouring states became alarmed.

The Sandinists' victory set off a regional chain reaction. It heartened the leftist guerrillas in El Salvador, who had long been resisting the country's military and rightist rulers; by 1980 a civil war had begun. The US accused Nicaragua of sending arms to the Salvadorean guerrillas across the Gulf of Fonseca. Nicaragua accused Honduras and Cost Rica of harbouring exile groups who were launching raids into Nicaragua. Meanwhile, in Guatemala, another long guerrilla struggle, marked by the army's brutal treatment of restive Indian peasants, had sent a stream of refugees fleeing into Mexico.

In the early 1980s the United States became more and more openly involved in supporting the 'contra' guerrillas in Nicaragua and putting pressure on the Sandinist regime there. At the same time it was pressing the neighbouring states to switch from military rule to elected governments: Honduras did so in 1981, El Salvador in 1984, Guatemala in 1985. (Costa Rica already had a civilian government – and a tradition of maintaining no army; Belize held free elections regularly, after independence, as it had done before.) In 1983 the 'Contadora group' (73) began to try to moderate the Central American conflicts. By 1987 US support for the 'contras' was becoming restricted (and the covert devices intended to maintain it had been exposed in the notorious 'Irangate' hearings). Then Costa Rica initiated a regional 'peace plan', to be carried out under UN and OAS supervision. One provision was for talks between El Salvador's government and its guerrilla leaders; these were duly held, in Geneva and elsewhere, but at the end of 1990 fighting was still going on.

In Nicaragua, however, the internationally supervised arrangements eventually bore fruit in 1990. An election was held in February, and the astonished Sandinists lost. The 'contras' were disarmed and disbanded. But, although the Sandinists allowed the new elected government to take office, they looted the treasury and other institutions before handing over, and they kept control of the army. The civilian government thus found that the generals were breathing down its neck – a familiar situation in Central America, indeed throughout Latin America (73).

70 Panama and Colombia

The isthmus of Panama was part of Colombia in 1902. In 1903 the United States proposed the building of a canal and, when Colombia was slow to agree, fomented a secession in Panama and prevented Colombia from suppressing it. Under a treaty then concluded with the new republic of Panama, the Americans built and operated the Panama Canal (6, 66), and garrisoned and controlled a ten-mile-wide zone along its banks. Three treaties that took effect in 1979 abolished the Canal Zone, gave Panama more say in the operation of the canal, and provided for Panama to take full control in the year 2000. An oil pipeline across Panama was completed in 1982.

General Manuel Noriega, Panama's military chief, made himself its effective ruler in 1984. He used a succession of figurehead presidents, but became more and more flagrant in rigging elections or simply ignoring their results. In 1987 the US halted aid and began to apply economic pressure; Noriega was indicted in the American courts on charges of helping Colombia's 'drug barons' to smuggle narcotics into the US. In December 1989 American forces occupied Panama. Noriega was taken to the US to face trial, and a new government was installed, representing the opposition groups which had won the 1989 election but had been kept out of power by Noriega and his soldiers.

In Colombia the production of cocaine (from coca grown in Peru and Bolivia as well as in Colombia) and smuggling to North American and European markets were becoming massive operations during the 1980s. (By some estimates, illegal South American cocaine production was about 100 tons in 1980 and five times as large in 1988, when its retail value was well over $20,000 million.) 'Drug barons' based in Medellin and Cali formed private armies, made deals with left-wing guerrilla groups, corrupted or killed policemen and terrorized some judges and politicians into blocking attempts to extradite drug traffickers to the US.

In August 1989 Colombia's government launched a new anti-drug drive, tracking down 'barons', killing some and extraditing others to the US; the gangs retaliated with a wave of murders, and over 1,000 violent deaths were reported in 12 months. The US applauded Colombia's action, and in February 1990 the presidents of Bolivia, Colombia, Peru and the US held

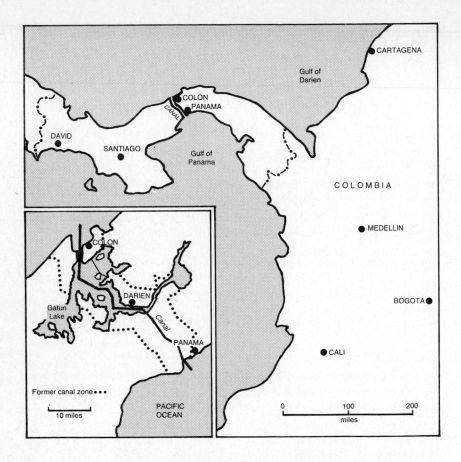

an 'anti-cocaine summit' meeting at Cartagena. But some US actions, such as the searching for drugs of ships stopped in Caribbean waters, aroused irritation. By the end of 1990 Colombia had a new president who was trying to get the 'barons' to surrender by promising them shorter prison terms and no extradition.

71 East Caribbean, Guianas

Between 1962 and 1981 Trinidad (with Tobago), Barbados, Grenada, Dominica, St Lucia, St Vincent and Antigua (with Barbuda) became independent – the last five having been, for a few years, 'associated states' whose defence and foreign relations remained in British hands (9). When St Kitts (with Nevis and Anguilla) became an associated state the 6,000 Anguillans threw off control from St Kitts, so in 1971 Britain took over Anguilla again, at the islanders' request. St Kitts (with Nevis) became independent in 1983. It was already a member of the Organization of Eastern Caribbean States (OECS), formed in 1981 by the smallest ex-British states.

The east Caribbean map thus shows an array of new sovereign states among the remaining American, British, Dutch and French islands. Puerto Rico is a self-governing 'commonwealth' attached to the United States. Guadeloupe (with St Barthélemy and part of St Martin) and Martinique are French overseas *départements*, as also is French Guiana (Guyane) on the mainland. Guyana (formerly British Guiana) and Surinam (ex-Dutch Guiana) became independent respectively in 1966 and 1975.

An old Venezuelan claim to more than half of Guyana – the whole area west of the Essequibo river – was revived in the 1980s; in 1987 the two governments sought the good offices of the UN secretary-general. Guyana had been troubled by its racial divisions; the ancestors of about half of its people came from Africa, half from southern Asia. Surinam has similar racial problems. Its soldiers seized power in 1980; by 1982 their repressive actions had led Holland to halt its economic aid; in 1988 a civilian government was installed and Dutch aid was resumed, but by then a third of the population had migrated to Holland, and others had fled into French Guiana. When the new government tried to negotiate an end to a 'Bush Negro' revolt the soldiers objected and began to interfere again; in 1990 they seized power for the second time.

In Grenada, a coup in 1979 installed a leftist regime which sought support from Cuba and broke its promise to hold elections. In 1983 its leaders quarrelled and it collapsed in bloody disarray. The OECS appealed for help, and troops from the US and six Caribbean islands landed in Grenada, meeting resistance mainly from armed Cubans. An

election in 1984 restored democratic government.

The other ex-British island states were able to hold free elections regularly. In Dominica in 1981 a coup was attempted with the help of foreign mercenaries; in Trinidad in 1990 a bid for power was made by a sect of self-styled 'Muslims' (unconnected with the island's many Muslims of south Asian origin). Both attempts were quickly suppressed.

72 Argentina and Falklands

In 1982 Argentina, then under military rule, seized the Falkland Islands and South Georgia. Within ten weeks all its occupying forces had surrendered to the counter-attacking British, but the conflict had brought Argentina world-wide attention. Its defeat also enabled the Argentines to make the humiliated generals' junta hand over to an elected civilian government in 1983.

Compared with most other Latin American countries, Argentina has a high national income per head. It has a large temperate zone, vast fertile plains, oil, gas, uranium (3, 4) and other mineral resources, and good communications. Its population – about 32 million – is almost entirely of European origin (with large Italian and German elements); after 175 years of independence it is not at all a typical 'third-world' country. Yet its production and living standards are far lower than those of Canada, a country that has comparable resources and population and a more severe climate. One explanation is that Argentina has suffered a sad amount of misgovernment, by most of its civilian rulers and all its many military ones.

Geography has shielded Argentina from external threats, and it remained lucratively neutral in the 1914–18 and 1939–45 wars (with a slant towards Nazi Germany in the second). Yet it has maintained large armed forces, which have carried out many coups (e.g. in 1930, 1943, 1955, 1966 and 1976) and have influenced politics even when not openly holding power. The country has often been able to dominate its smaller neighbours, and military regimes in Bolivia and Paraguay have had support from Buenos Aires, whose influence has at times reached much farther north.

In recent years, expansionist ideas in Argentina have also been turned towards the south. After the exploitation of oilfields in previously undeveloped Patagonia, hopes of offshore oil have increased interest in the waters around Cape Horn, the Falklands, other southern islands and the Antarctic continent. Like other signatories of the 1959 Antarctic Treaty (12), Argentina has agreed not to press its claims south of latitude 60°South for the time being, but some of its actions have indicated that it wants to strengthen those claims with an eye to the future. Argentina and Chile, whose Antarctic claims overlap, tend to use their armed forces to staff their 'demilitarized' research bases, and to fly wives in to give birth there to

Argentina's claims

future citizens who, being Antarctic-born, may be offered as 'living evidence' in support of territorial claims some day.

The introduction of 200-mile sea zones (6) intensified Argentina's old quarrel with Chile over the three small islands, Lennox, Nueva and Picton, at the eastern end of the Beagle Channel, south of Tierra del Fuego, because possession of these islands could determine the control of large adjacent areas of sea. Although this was often called 'the Beagle Channel dispute', the channel (named from the famous voyage in the 1830s of the British survey ship HMS *Beagle*, with Charles Darwin aboard) was not itself contested; part of its course is a recognized frontier, the rest is within Chile's territory.

In 1977 five judges of the International Court, to whom the case had been referred for arbitration, gave a decision under which Chile would retain the three islands, and other islands farther south, including the one

on which Cape Horn is situated. Argentina rejected these terms and seemed about to go to war, but after some tense months it agreed to refer the dispute to the Pope. His proposals, presented in 1980, resembled the judges', and again Argentina refused to end the dispute. However, in 1984, after Argentina's defeat in the Falklands and its consequent switch from military to civilian government, a treaty was concluded. The Pope's original terms had been slightly changed, but without any real swing to either side. Chile thus kept the islands, and a sea dividing line running south from Cape Horn was accepted.

The Falkland Islands (in Spanish, Malvinas) were uninhabited until small settlements were founded by the French (1764), the British (1766) and the Spanish (1767). The French renounced their claims and left; Britain withdrew its garrison in 1774 but maintained its claims; Spain abandoned the islands in 1810. Argentina made a claim to them in the 1820s but failed to take effective control. Britain reasserted its claims, effectively, in 1833, and the little British colony was soon thriving, servicing ships on voyages around Cape Horn. Later, steamships, which normally took the Magellan Strait route through Chile, made Punta Arenas their usual port of call; Port Stanley lost business, but sheep farming continued to support a population of about 2,000, almost all of British origin.

Argentina maintained its claims, and found support in Latin America for its 'anti-colonial' arguments. Talks were held, in which Britain – having promised the islanders that sovereignty would not be transferred without their consent – tried to focus on economic co-operation; but in 1977 it agreed to discuss sovereignty too. In April 1982 Argentina abruptly interrupted the talks by landing 14,000 soldiers on the Falklands and South Georgia. When attempts to negotiate a withdrawal failed, the British counter-attacked, quickly recapturing South Georgia and forcing the Argentine troops in the Falklands to surrender by mid-June. The British task force had been operating at extreme range – Ascension Island, 3,400 miles to the north, having the nearest airfield and staging point available to it.

Britain then found itself having to keep an expensive garrison in the Falklands, and to build an airfield fit for long-range airliners. In 1986, however, it proclaimed a 150 mile wide fishery zone around the islands (6), and this brought the Falklands large revenues from foreign fishing fleets, which now had to buy permits. In 1990 Britain and Argentina restored diplomatic relations and reached other agreements about joint action to control fishing in the waters between the mainland and the Falklands. But there was an uneasy background to these developments: since 1983 discontented army officers had made several attempts to bring down, or browbeat, Argentina's civilian governments. The military establishment was still powerful enough to shield many officers from prosecution for atrocities against Argentine civilians committed during the 1976–83 period of military rule.

73 Latin America

Brazil represents what was once Portugal's empire in the Americas. The former Spanish empire there is represented by the 18 Spanish-speaking (Hispanic) republics; they include two in the Caribbean, Cuba and the Dominican Republic. Haiti was once a French possession. These 20 Latin republics, with the United States, were members of the Pan-American Union, which was succeeded in 1948 by the Organization of American States (OAS). Since the 1960s the CAS has suspended Cuba from membership and has been joined by Canada, the ex-British Caribbean states and Surinam. The 1947 Rio Treaty (Inter-American Treaty of Reciprocal Assistance), concluded by the 20 Latin states and the USA, provided for joint action if any member was attacked. Argentina invoked the treaty during the 1982 Falklands conflict (72) but got little response.

Regional economic integration has made little progress. In 1960 Mexico and the ten Latin states of South America founded the Latin American Free Trade Association (LAFTA), with the aim of creating a common market. In 1980 the same 11 states agreed to relaunch the effort, and renamed their grouping the Latin American Integration Association (LAIA), but progress remained modest. In the early 1960s only 8% of Latin American states' exports went to other states in the region; in the late 1980s the figure had reached only 11%. The 1969 Andean Pact, signed by Bolivia, Chile, Colombia, Ecuador and Peru, and later by Venezuela, was aimed at drawing together a smaller group, as were two other projects launched in the 1960s: the five-member Central American common market (due for relaunching in 1991); and the Caribbean Free Trade Association, formed by the new ex-British states, which developed into the Caribbean Community (Caricom) and made a start on diplomatic as well as economic co-operation.

In 1984 11 Latin governments formed the 'Cartagena group', for consultations about their problem of heavy foreign debts. This problem, intensified in the late 1970s by over-eager borrowing, through banks, of the huge sums that some OPEC countries piled up after the big oil price rises of the 1970s (3), was not confined to Latin America, but Brazil and Mexico alone owed about $200,000 million – more than a fifth of total third-world debt – and it was Mexico which, in 1982, dramatized the problem when it announced that it could not keep up payments on its debts.

The 'Contadora group', formed in 1983 at a meeting on an island near

USA

MEXICO

Mexico City

Bermuda (Br)

CUBA

BELIZE
HONDURAS

GUATEMALA
EL SALVADOR

JAMAICA

DOMINICAN
REPUBLIC

NICARAGUA

HAITI

COSTA RICA   Cartagena

PANAMA

BARBADOS

TRINIDAD AND TOBAGO

VENEZUELA

Bogota

GUYANA

COLOMBIA

SURINAM

ECUADOR   Quito

FRENCH GUIANA

Amazon

EQUATOR

Lima   PERU

BRAZIL

La Paz

Arica   BOLIVIA

Brasilia

CHILE   PARAGUAY

Asuncion

Sao
Paulo

Rio de
Janeiro

Santiago

ARGENTINA   ANDES

Buenos
Aires

URUGUAY
Montevideo

Viedma

Falklands

0   miles   1000

0   km   1000

Cape Horn

216

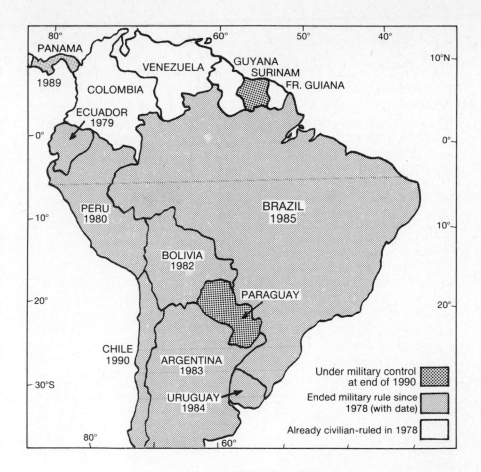

Panama, comprised Colombia, Mexico, Panama and Venezuela, which
came together to try to moderate the conflicts among the Central American
states (*69*). In 1986 Argentina, Brazil, Peru and Uruguay formed a 'support
group' for the original four, and the combined 'Group of Eight' began to
hold meetings to discuss economic and other problems.

One obstacle to regional unity is the persistence of old territorial
disputes. There has been no recent war comparable to the 1932–5 one
between Bolivia and Paraguay (the 'Chaco war', so named from the
disputed area). But Argentina and Chile had a long quarrel over the Beagle
Channel islands; in the mid-1980s Nicaragua revived an old claim to
Colombia's San Andres islands; and Venezuela still has claims on part of
Guyana (*69, 71, 72*). In 1942, after a short war, Ecuador had to cede territory

217

to Peru; in 1961 it declared that it would no longer respect the 1942 treaty; in 1981 and 1984 there were clashes on the frontier (the revival of this dispute was linked with both countries' search for oil).

Ever since the 1879–83 'War of the Pacific', in which Chile defeated Bolivia and Peru and took from them the mineral-rich coastal area running south from Arica, Bolivia has hoped to regain an outlet to the sea (it still maintains a navy). In 1975 Chile offered it an outlet in exchange for an inland area; but Peru objected, and the negotiations broke down, as did a new round of talks in 1987.

The 1967 Treaty of Tlatelolco (named from a mountain near Mexico City) was designed to make Latin America a zone free of nuclear weapons. But in 1990 the treaty was still not in full force with regard to Argentina, Brazil, Chile or Cuba (4).

Recent years have seen a widespread return to civilian rule by elected governments, after a period in which military regimes had been predominant. Between 1979 and 1985 military rulers handed over to civilians in Argentina, Bolivia, Brazil, Ecuador, Peru and Uruguay – and, in Central America (69), in El Salvador, Honduras and Guatemala. In 1990 Chile followed suit. Paraguay remained under military rule (although a 1989 coup ousted General Alfredo Stroessner, who had ruled for 34 years). In 1990 Surinam reverted to military rule, and Panama was freed from it by a US invasion (70, 71). The civilian governments, however, often found that they had to take account of the views of army officers who had not lost their taste for power. These views were not always right-wing: in Nicaragua the leftist Sandinists, although defeated in the 1990 election, kept control of the armed forces and thus could put strong pressure on the new government.

Appendix: Countries and currencies

CFA: African Financial Community (mostly ex-French states); CFP: French Pacific Community.

Africa

Algeria	Algerian dinar
Angola	Kwanza
Benin	CFA franc
Botswana	Pula
Burkina Faso	CFA franc
Burundi	Burundi franc
Cameroun	CFA franc
Cape Verde	Cape Verde escudo
Central African Republic	CFA franc
Chad	CFA franc
Comoros	Comoros franc
Congo	CFA franc
Djibouti	Djibouti franc
Egypt	Egyptian pound
Equatorial Guinea	CFA franc
Ethiopia	Birr
Gabon	CFA franc
The Gambia	Dalasi
Ghana	Cedi
Guinea	Guinea franc
Guinea-Bissau	Guinea-Bissau peso
Ivory Coast	CFA franc
Kenya	Kenya shilling
Lesotho	Loti
Liberia	Liberian dollar and US dollar
Libya	Libyan dinar
Madagascar	Malagasy franc
Malawi	Malawi kwacha
Mali	CFA franc
Mauritania	Ouguiya
Mauritius	Mauritius rupee
Mayotte	French franc
Morocco	Morocco dirham
Mozambique	Metical

Namibia	Namibia rand
Niger	CFA franc
Nigeria	Naira
Réunion	French franc
Rwanda	Rwanda franc
Sao Tomé and Principe	Dobra
Senegal	CFA franc
Seychelles	Seychelles rupee
Sierra Leone	Leone
Somalia	Somalia shilling
South Africa	Rand
Sudan	Sudan pound
Swaziland	Lilangeni
Tanzania	Tanzania shilling
Togo	CFA franc
Tunisia	Tunisia dinar
Uganda	Uganda shilling
Zaire	Zaire
Zambia	Zambia kwacha
Zimbabwe	Zimbabwe dollar

The Americas

Anguilla	East Caribbean dollar
Antigua and Barbuda	East Caribbean dollar
Argentina	Austral
Aruba	Aruba guilder
Bahamas	Bahamas dollar
Barbados	Barbados dollar
Belize	Belize dollar
Bermuda	Bermuda dollar
Bolivia	Boliviano
Brazil	Cruzado
Canada	Canadian dollar
Cayman Islands	Cayman Islands dollar
Chile	Chile peso
Colombia	Colombia peso
Costa Rica	Costa Rica colon
Cuba	Cuba peso
Dominica	East Caribbean dollar
Dominican Republic	Dominican Republic peso
Ecuador	Sucre
El Salvador	El Salvador colon
Falkland Islands	Pound sterling
French Guiana	French franc
Grenada	East Caribbean dollar
Guadeloupe	French franc

Guatemala	Quetzal
Guyana	Guyana dollar
Haiti	Gourde
Honduras	Lempira
Jamaica	Jamaica dollar
Martinique	French franc
Mexico	Mexican peso
Montserrat	East Caribbean dollar
Netherlands Antilles (Curaçao, etc.)	Netherlands Antilles guilder
Nicaragua	Cordoba
Panama	Balboa and US dollar
Paraguay	Guarani
Peru	Inti
Puerto Rico	US dollar
St Kitts and Nevis	East Caribbean dollar
St Lucia	East Caribbean dollar
St Vincent	East Caribbean dollar
Surinam	Surinam guilder
Trinidad and Tobago	Trinidad and Tobago dollar
Turks and Caicos Islands	US dollar
United States	US dollar
Uruguay	Uruguay new peso
Venezuela	Bolivar
Virgin Islands (British)	US dollar
Virgin Islands (US)	US dollar

Asia

Afghanistan	Afghani
Bahrain	Bahrain dinar
Bangladesh	Taka
Bhutan	Ngultrum
Brunei	Brunei dollar
Burma (Myanmar)	Kyat
Cambodia (Kampuchea)	Riel
China	Yuan
Hong Kong	Hong Kong dollar
India	Indian rupee
Indonesia	Rupiah
Iran	Rial
Iraq	Iraqi dinar
Israel	New sheqel
Japan	Yen
Jordan	Jordan dinar
Korean (North)	North Korea won
Korea (South)	South Korea won
Kuwait	Kuwait dinar

Laos	Kip
Lebanon	Lebanon pound
Malaysia	Ringgit
Maldives	Rufiyaa
Mongolia	Tugrik
Nepal	Nepal rupee
Oman	Oman rial
Pakistan	Pakistan rupee
Philippines	Philippines peso
Qatar	Qatar riyal
Saudi Arabia	Saudi riyal
Singapore	Singapore dollar
Sri Lanka	Sri Lanka rupee
Syria	Syria pound
Taiwan	Taiwan new dollar
Thailand	Baht
United Arab Emirates	UAE dirham
Vietnam	New dong
Yemen	Yemen rial

Europe

Albania	Lek
Andorra	French franc and Spanish peseta
Austria	Schilling
Baltic states	Soviet rouble
Belgium	Belgian franc
Bulgaria	Lev
Cyprus	Cyprus pound and Turkish lira
Czechoslovakia	Koruna
Denmark	Krone
Faroes	Faroes krone
Finland	Markka (Finnmark)
France	French franc
Germany	Deutschmark
Gibraltar	Pound sterling
Greece	Drachma
Hungary	Forint
Iceland	Kröna
Ireland	Punt (pound)
Italy	Italian lira
Jugoslavia	Jugoslav dinar
Liechtenstein	Swiss franc
Luxembourg	Luxembourg franc
Malta	Maltese pound (lira)
Monaco	French franc
Netherlands (Holland)	Dutch guilder

Norway	Norwegian krone
Poland	Zloty
Portugal	Escudo
Rumania	Leu
San Marino	Italian lira
Soviet Union (USSR)	Rouble
Spain	Peseta
Sweden	Krona
Switzerland	Swiss franc
Turkey	Turkish lira
United Kingdom (Britain)	Pound sterling
Vatican State (Holy See)	Italian lira

The Pacific (Oceania)

Australia	Australian dollar
Cook Islands	Cook Islands dollar
Fiji	Fiji dollar
French Polynesia	CFP franc
Guam	US dollar
Kiribati	Australian dollar
Micronesia	US dollar
Nauru	Australian dollar
New Caledonia	CFP franc
New Zealand	New Zealand dollar
Niue	New Zealand dollar
Papua New Guinea	Kina
Pitcairn	New Zealand dollar
Samoa (American)	US dollar
Samoa (Western)	Tala
Solomon Islands	Solomon Islands dollar
Tokelau	New Zealand dollar
Tonga	Pa'anga
Tuvalu	Tuvalu dollar
Vanuatu	Vatu
Wallis and Futuna	CFP franc

Index

Each number refers to a section (map and/or accompanying notes), not to a page. Former names are shown in brackets, eg Annaba (*Bone*). Where appropriate, the principal entry is shown in **bold**.

Ogasawara *see* Bonins
oil 2, **3**, 40; of Aegean region 26; of
    Antarctica 12; and Arab–Israeli conflict
    43; of Arctic region 11, 22; of Argentina
    72; of Australasia 64; of Canada 68; of
    Gulf states 46; of Iraq 45, 48; for Japan
    40, 41, 57; and north–south divide 7;
    offshore 6, 22; of Saudi Arabia 45; of
    Soviet Union 15, 22; of United States 67
Okinawa 57, 66
Omaha 67
Oman 3, 29, 40, 41, 45, 46
Omsk 15, 53
Ontario 68
opium trade 59
Oran (Wahran) 38
Orange Free State 33
Oranjemund 34
Organization of African unity (OAU) 30, 37,
    39
Organization of American States (OAS) 69,
    73
Organization of Arab Petroleum Exporting
    Countries (OAPEC) 40
Organization of Eastern Caribbean States
    (OECS) 71
Organization for Economic Co-operation
    and Development (OECD) 19
Organization for European Economic Co-
    operation (OEEC) 19
Organization of Petroleum Exporting
    Countries (OPEC) 3, 7, 40
Orissa, Oriya 51
Orkney islands 22
Ottawa 68
Ovambo 34
Ovimbundu 34
Oxus *see* Amu Darya
ozone layer 1, 12

Pacific Ocean 65, 66
Padang 63
Pahlavi, Shah Mohammed Reza 47
Pakistan 1, 3, 4, 8, 9, 23, 27, 28, 45, 49, **50, 51**,
    52, 59
Palatinate *see* Pfalz
Palau (Belau) 65
Palawan 62
Palestine 8, **42, 43**
Palestine Liberation Organization (PLO)
    29, 42, 43, 44
Pamirs 49, 53
Panama 69, **70**

Panama Canal 6, **70**
Panjshir 49
Panmunjom 58
Paphos 26
Papua New Guinea (PNG) 9, **63**, 65
Paracels 54
Paraguay 73
Paramaribo 71
Patagonia 72
Pathans 49, 50
Pearl Harbor 66
Pearl river 56
Pechenga (Petsamo) 14, 21
Peking *see* Beijing
Penang 62
Penghu (Pescadores) 55
Pentagonal 17
Perim 45
Perpetual Maritime Truce (1853) 46
Persia *see* Iran
Persian Gulf *see* Gulf
Pescadores (Penghu) 55
Peshawar 49
Petsamo (Pechenga) 14, 21
Pfalz (Palatinate) 18
Philippines 54, 57, **59**, 60, 62, 66
Phnom Penh 60, 61
phosphate reserves 39, 65
pipelines, oil **40**, 45, 48
Pitcairn 9, 65
Plate (Rio de la Plata) 72
platinum reserves 5
plutonium reprocessing 4
Poland 12–16, 18, 21
Polisario guerillas 38, 39
pollution 1, 4, 6
Polynesia 64, 65
Pomaks 16
Pomerania 18
Pondicherry 50
population 1; of Africa 30; of Canada 68; of
    United States 67
Porkkala 21
Port Arthur (Canada) *see* Thunder Bay
Port Arthur (China) 53
Port Elizabeth 33
Port Moresby 63
Port Said 42
Port of Spain 71
Port Stanley 72
Portugal 4, 19, 20; and Africa 27, 30–4, 36;
    and Americas 73; and Far East 27, 56, 63
power resources 2; in Australasia 64; of

235